EDITOR:

 OSPREY MILITARY MEN-AT

EL CID AND THE RECONQUISTA 1050-1492

Text by
DAVID NICOLLE PhD
Colour plates by
ANGUS McBRIDE

Dedication

For Dr. Ada Bruhn de Hoffmeyer,
Instituto de Estudios Sobre
Armas Antiguas, Jarandilla.

First published in Great Britain in 1988 by
Osprey Publishing, Elms Court, Chapel Way, Botley,
Oxford OX2 9LP, United Kingdom.
Email: info@ospreypublishing.com

British Library Cataloguing in Publication Data

Nicolle, David
   El Cid and the Reconquista.—(Men-at-arms
series; 200).
   1. Spain. Military operations, 1000–1500
I. Title   II. Series
355.4′0946

   ISBN 0-85045-840-4

Filmset in Great Britain
Printed in China through World Print Ltd.

FOR A CATALOGUE OF ALL BOOKS PUBLISHED BY
OSPREY MILITARY, AUTOMOTIVE AND AVIATION
PLEASE WRITE TO:

The Marketing Manager, Osprey Direct USA, PO Box 130,
Sterling Heights, MI 48311-0130, USA.
Email: info@ospreydirectusa.com

The Marketing Manager, Osprey Direct UK, PO Box 140,
Wellingborough, Northants, NN8 4ZA, United Kingdom.
Email: info@ospreydirect.co.uk

VISIT OSPREY AT
www.ospreypublishing.com

Artist's Note

The artist wishes to dedicate the colour plates in this
book to the memory of the late Ronald Embleton.

Readers may care to note that the original paintings
from which the colour plates in this book were
prepared are available for private sale. All
reproduction copyright whatsoever is retained by the
Publishers. All enquiries should be addressed to:

Scorpio Gallery
PO Box 475,
Hailsham,
E. Sussex BN27 2SL

The Publishers regret that they can enter into no
correspondence upon this matter.

El Cid and the Reconquista

Introduction

The very name *El Cid* sums up much of the special character of medieval Spanish warfare. It comes from the Arabic *al sayyid*, master or chieftain, and seems to have been given to Rodrigo de Vivar by his Muslim foes. But was it given in recognition of El Cid's victories against Islam in the 'Reconquista'—or because this Castilian nobleman was as content to serve beside the Muslims as to fight them?

Rodrigo de Vivar came from the lesser nobility of Castile. He was not one of the great magnates, and his successes were sometimes distasteful to such barons. The popular view sees El Cid as a Christian champion whose early victories gave leadership of Spain to Castile rather than Leon, but who was then exiled to Aragon through the machinations of his rivals. El Cid was supposedly obsessed with the idea of a unified Spain and the defeat of the 'Moors', while his capture and government of Muslim Valencia is portrayed as an example of cultural harmony under Christian leadership. He is also believed to have halted the Almoravid, African (and consequently barbarian) tide which threatened to engulf Spain.

Another view of El Cid comes from those who study the civilisation of *al Andalus* (Muslim Spain and Portugal), some of whom note his acceptance of Arab-Andalusian culture, and portray him almost as an Andalusian rather than Spanish hero. Perhaps El Cid was simply an adventurer, one of many seen on the turbulent Christian-Muslim frontier, comparable to the Portuguese Giraldo Sempavor—who seized the Muslim city of Badajoz in the 1160s, only to lose it to the Almohades just as El Cid's followers lost Valencia to the Almoravids.

The story of the Reconquista, or the Christian conquest of the Iberian peninsula, is a classic case of history being written by the winning side. For hundreds of years the Muslim period was dismissed

Beatus Commentaries on the Apocalypse, 1091–1109. In this Mozarab manuscript an angel fights the Beast, wielding a sword with a trilobate pommel and wearing an outer garment of large pieces of heavy material stitched together—perhaps of buff leather. (Ms. Add. 11695, British Lib., London.)

3

'The Betrayal', carved capital late 12th C. Note the small kite-shaped shields, (*in situ* Monastery of las Huelgas, Burgos).

as an alien interlude, the Muslim Andalusians simply being conquerors justly reconquered. In fact these Andalusians were of mixed origin. The Muslims were descended from local converts, Arab and Berber immigrants, and northern or eastern European slaves. Those who had remained Christian were called Mozarabs; and there was also a sizeable Jewish population. Family and tribal divisions were now political rather than ethnic, the entire community being Arabised in culture, though generally speaking an early form of Spanish in their homes. By the 11th century the local élite was largely demilitarised, the army being drawn almost entirely from European slaves and 'new' Berbers from North Africa (see MAA 125 *The Armies of Islam 7th–11th Centuries*). Small wonder that when the Umayyad Caliphate of Cordova collapsed early in the 11th century, it was the Berber and Slav army which fought over the pieces. In 1031 the Berbers and their puppet Caliph were defeated, and Andalus fragmented into numerous petty states known as *taifa* kingdoms.

Meanwhile the situation among the almost equally fragmented states of the Christian north was changing. Each faced different problems. The king of Aragon had been politically weak and chronically short of money since the 10th century. Urban militias appeared as early as the 9th century in Leon, and were certainly a major feature in 11th century Castile. Such forces included mounted *caballeros* and infantry *peons. Caballeros* were summoned more often than *peons* while southern frontier cities faced heavier military burdens than those in the north. The 11th and 12th centuries were a time of population expansion in Christian Europe, and northern Spain was soon relatively overpopulated (though the cities of the Muslim south were still much bigger than those of the Christian north). Christian confidence and aggression was also seen in the Iberian peninsula. Yet there was no real Crusading attitude before the 12th century, and even then religious motives were often secondary to political or economic calculations.

In this explosive situation warfare was dominated by mountain ranges and great rivers which tended to provide defensive frontiers, while a road system created by the Romans and extended by the Muslims channelled major campaigns. Spain's fierce climate also meant that most fighting took place in summer or autumn. Castles varied greatly in size, some defending bridges, fords or passes while the biggest served as major operational bases. Castles were not, however, the target of expansion: cities were the goal of all conquerors, their seizure usually following years of raiding, the destruction of surrounding agriculture, a blockade of trade and finally a siege.

Iberian warfare differed from that of the rest of western Europe in its emphasis on light cavalry, light infantry (including archers), a lack of body armour and on raiding rather than pitched battles. As the Christians pushed south of the sierras and onto the high plains, long-distance raiding *cabalgadas* by cavalry forces increased in importance. The peninsula had, of course, been a cavalry arena since the time of the Ibero-Celts.[1] Their tactics of repeated attack and retreat can be compared to the Roman *cursores et defensores*, the Arab *karr wa farr* and the later Spanish *torno fuya*. Of course these traditions were constantly refined, the spread of

[1] See MAA 180, *Rome's Enemies (4): Spanish Armies, 218 BC–19 BC.*

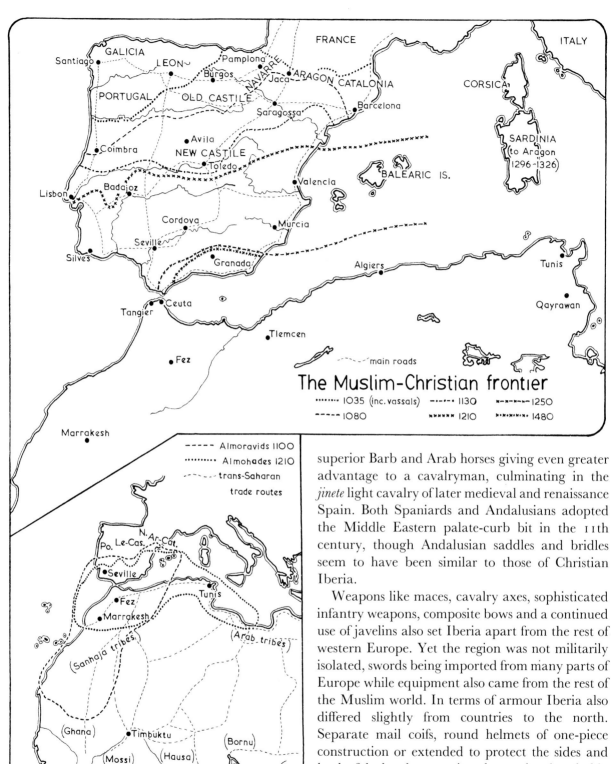

GALICIA
Santiago
LEON
PORTUGAL
OLD CASTILE
Coimbra
Lisbon
Badajoz
Silves
Seville
Cordova
Granada
Tangier
Ceuta
Fez
Marrakesh
FRANCE
Pamplona
Burgos
NAVARRE
Jaca
ARAGON
CATALONIA
Saragossa
Barcelona
Avila
NEW CASTILE
Toledo
Valencia
BALEARIC IS.
Murcia
Algiers
Tlemcen
ITALY
CORSICA
SARDINIA
(to Aragon
1296-1326)
Tunis
Qayrawan

main roads

The Muslim-Christian frontier

| ·········· 1035 (inc. vassals) | ------- 1130 | ·—·—·— 1250 |
| ----- 1080 | ×××××× 1210 | ·×·×·×· 1480 |

---- Almoravids 1100
········ Almohades 1210
-·-·- trans-Saharan
        trade routes

Po. Le-Cas.
N. Ar-Cat.
Seville
Fez
Tunis
Marrakesh
(Sanhaja tribes)
(Arab tribes)
(Ghana)
Timbuktu
(Bornu)
(Mossi)
(Hausa)

superior Barb and Arab horses giving even greater advantage to a cavalryman, culminating in the *jinete* light cavalry of later medieval and renaissance Spain. Both Spaniards and Andalusians adopted the Middle Eastern palate-curb bit in the 11th century, though Andalusian saddles and bridles seem to have been similar to those of Christian Iberia.

Weapons like maces, cavalry axes, sophisticated infantry weapons, composite bows and a continued use of javelins also set Iberia apart from the rest of western Europe. Yet the region was not militarily isolated, swords being imported from many parts of Europe while equipment also came from the rest of the Muslim world. In terms of armour Iberia also differed slightly from countries to the north. Separate mail coifs, round helmets of one-piece construction or extended to protect the sides and back of the head were quite advanced and probably betrayed Middle Eastern influence. On the other hand iron helmets were rare and expensive in the Christian states, while hardened leather defences seem to have been widespread on both sides of the frontier. The hide coats mentioned in some sources

Carved portal, 12th C. Here two identical knights have shields and helmets but no body armour or coifs (*in situ* church, Artaiz, Navarre).

were probably of buff leather, though hardened *cuir bouilli* lamellar of Eastern inspiration may have been known. Some Christian sources speak of 'Moors' wearing 'cordwain' but this was a soft leather originally made in Cordova, and probably referred to light leather clothing worn by some North Africans.

Other regional peculiarities included, on the Christian side, a custom of raising newly proclaimed leaders on two spear-shafts, and a strong, almost anti-feudal clan spirit which echoed the supposed tribalism of Andalus. To the south the Andalusian élite had adopted Egyptian rather than Berber fashions, but showed a strong reluctance to wear turbans, these being reserved for religious leaders, while the military sported scarlet capes inspired by the Spanish *capa*.

Chronology

(Main Muslim-Christian conflicts in *italics*)

1031	End of Umayyad Caliphate in Andalus; fragmentation into '*taifa*' petty states.
1040s	Formation of Almoravid movement in western Sahara.
1052–7	Fragmentation of North Africa.
1054	Almoravids raid Ghana.
1055–65	*'Taifa' states tributary to King-Emperor of Castile-Leon.*
1064	*Capture of Coimbra by Portugal.*
1065	Civil war in Castile-Leon.
c.1069	Almoravids conquer Morocco.
1082	Almoravids capture Algiers.
1085	*Capture of Toledo by Castile*; Muslims ask Almoravids for aid.
1086	*Almoravids defeat Castile-Leon at Zallaka.*
1086–91	Almoravids conquer Andalus.
1094	*El Cid seizes Valencia.*
1097	*Almoravids defeat Castile at Consuegra and Cuenca*; autonomy of Portugal recognised by Leon.
1099	*Almoravids besiege El Cid in Valencia, death of El Cid.*
1108	*Almoravids defeat Christians at Ucles.*
1110	Almoravids capture Saragossa from last '*taifa*' king.
1118	*Capture of Saragossa by Aragon.*
1120s	Formation of Almohade movement in Morocco.
1121	Anti-Almoravid revolt in Cordova.
1125	*Castile ravages Andalus.*
1127	Leon invades Portugal.
1135	King of Leon recognised as overlord of

Navarre and Aragon.

1139	*Portuguese defeat Almoravids at Ourique.*
c.1141–7	Almohades defeat Almoravids, capture Marrakesh.
1143	Full independence of Portugal.
1146–9	*Capture of Tunisian coast by Normans of Sicily.*
1147	Almohades capture Seville, Almoravides flee to Majorca.
	Capture of Lisbon by Portugal and English Crusaders.
1150	Almohades recognised as rulers of Andalus.
1152	Almohades conquer Algeria.
1159	*Almohades drive Normans from Tunisian coast.*
1170–80	Intermittent war between Leon and Castile.
1172	*Almohades capture Murcia.*
1179	Castile and Aragon agree future partition of Andalus.
1184	*Almohades defeated at Santarem.*
1195	*Almohades defeat Castile at Alarcos; Almoravids of Majorca seize Tunisia.*
1203	Almohades conquer Majorca from Almoravids.
1205–7	Almohades defeat Almoravids in Tunisia.
1212	*Christian alliance defeats Almohades at Las Navas de Tolosa.*
1227	Almohade civil war and conflict with Marinids.
1228	Foundation of Hafsid dynasty in Tunisia.
1229–35	*Capture of Majorca by Aragon.*
1230	Final reunion of Leon and Castile.
1230s	Ibn Hud controls most of Andalus; Ziyanid dynasty in Algeria.
1233	*Castile defeats Granada at Jerez.*
1236	*Capture of Cordova by Castile.*
1236–49	*Capture of Algarve by Portugal.*
1238	*Capture of Valencia by Aragon.*
1246	*Granada vassal of Castile.*
1247–58	*Muslim revolt in southern Valencia.*

Gate of Al Jaferiya Palace, Saragossa, 1046–81. This fortress is of typical Andalusian stone (towers) and brick (walls) construction, and is in a tradition dating back to the early Islamic period in Syria.

1248	*Capture of Seville by Castile*; foundation of Nasrid dynasty in Granada.
1250	Marinid dynasty at Fes, Morocco.
1252–1310	Periodic civil wars in Castile.
1264–7	*Muslim revolt in Andalusia.*
1269	Extinction of Almohades by Marinids.
1270	*King Louis of France invades Tunisia, defeated.*
1275–85	*Four Marinid expeditions to Spain.*
1276–80	*Muslim revolt in Valencia.*
1282–3	Aragonese conquest of Sicily.
1285	War between France and Aragon-Catalonia.
1291	Castile and Aragon agree partition of North Africa in expectation of conquest.
1292	*Castile captures Tarifa from Marinids.*
1295–1302	Civil wars in Castile.
1310	*Castile captures Gibraltar.*
1319	*Castilian invasion defeated outside Granada.*
1324	Catalonia occupies Sardinia.
1333	*Gibraltar retaken by Granada.*
1337	Marinids capture Tlemcen.
1340	*Castilian fleet defeated by Marinids off Algeciras; Marinid invasion defeated at Salado; capture of Algeciras by Castile.*
1341	Portuguese raid Canary Islands.
1347–9	Marinid occupation of Tunisia.
1358	Marinids lose Tlemcen.
1367	Civil war in Castile, Anglo-Castilians defeat Franco-Castilians at Najera.
1373	Anglo-Portuguese treaty signed 'for ever'.
1385	Anglo-Portuguese defeat of Castilian invasion at Aljubarrota.
1402	French adventurers occupy Canaries in name of Castile.
1410	*Castile captures Antequera from Granada.*
1415	*Capture of Ceuta by Portuguese.*
1420	Portuguese occupation of Madeira.
1435	Aragon defeated by Genoese.
1431–45	Portuguese occupation of Azores.
1445	Rebel nobility of Castile defeated by royalists at Olmedo.
1449	Portuguese civil war.
1458–91	*Capture of Moroccan Atlantic ports by Portuguese.*
1462	*Gibraltar again captured by Castile.*
1469	Marriage of Ferdinand Prince of Aragon and Isabella Princess of Castile.
1470s	Full Castilian conquest of Canaries.
1474–9	Civil war between Castilian-Portuguese alliance and Castilian-Aragonese alliance; victory of Castilian-Aragonese leads to unification of Castile-Aragon under Ferdinand and Isabella.
1482–92	*Castile-Aragon conquers kingdom of Granada*; expulsion of Jews in Castile-Aragon.
1502	Expulsion of Spanish Muslims in violation of 1492 surrender terms.

Carved basin called the *Pila*, probably from a palace early-mid 11th C. Here two apparently unarmoured horsemen fight with broad-bladed spears. (Archaeol. Museum, Jativa, courtesy of L. A. Mayer Inst., Jerusalem.)

Christian Armies 1050-1150

The loose feudal structure of Spanish military organisation is reflected in troubadour epics of the period, including the *Poema del Cid*. Even the area's frontiers, particularly those between Christendom and Islam, were not very rigidly defined, each side holding towns while the heavily raided zone between fell to whoever was stronger at the time.

On the other hand French military influence was now felt, most strongly in Catalonia. A cavalry élite adopted the tall saddle, straight-legged riding position and couched lance of typical 12th century knights, plus shock-cavalry tactics of close-packed formations designed to break enemy ranks by weight or momentum. Mail hauberks became more common, though scale armour probably remained in use and may indicate a survival of Arab-Islamic ideas. Quilted armour was certainly used, either alone or with mail, and clearly reflected Islamic influence. Brightly coloured cloaks were a mark of the military class but were normally removed before combat. The adoption of 'modern' cavalry tactics was not always an advantage, however. The difficulty of remounting when using a tall saddle and long stirrup landed many a horseman in trouble when facing lighter and more agile Muslim cavalry.

Another, perhaps more significant military development was the widespread adoption of crossbows during the 11th century: Spaniards probably led the way but Andalusians were only a few years behind. As elsewhere in Europe this led to a decline in ordinary archery; yet for various reasons, such as the remoteness of some regions and continued influence from North Africa, simple archery survived right up to the 15th century. Morale and fighting spirit were strengthened by a *cantador* who rode ahead of the troops, singing heroic tales such as that of El Cid.

The Christian offensive which began in the mid-11th century followed the tradition of earlier wars and involved two forms of campaign. First there were raids of varying magnitude designed to seize valuables, livestock and prisoners; such expeditions were carried out by mounted troops, and were of limited duration. Then there were longer-term campaigns intended to seize and hold territory;

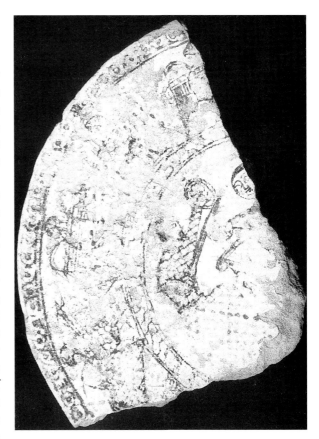

Ceramic wall-plaque from the Sabra Palace, Tunisia, mid-11th C. It shows a bearded infantryman with sword, small round shield and perhaps quilted armour facing a beardless horseman. (Bardo Museum, Tunis.)

more troops were involved, and naturally included infantry, siege engineers, baggage trains and the wherewithal to resist counter-attack. Muslim armies operated in the same way and both sides developed systems to exchange or ransom prisoners. By the 1130s Christian frontier towns incorporated such regulations in their charters and most of the Military Orders also had special centres for this purpose. Early in the 13th century a special Order of St. Mary of Mercy was created specifically to negotiate ransoms. Muslim, Christian and Jewish doctors served on both sides, while towns built hospitals to care for the wounded. Such concerns may have made Iberian warfare more civilised than elsewhere in Europe, but there were many darker sides.

Leon

By the 12th century the Spanish kingdoms assumed that a total Reconquista was inevitable. Each kingdom claimed legal descent from the Visigothic state overthrown by Muslim Arabs in the 8th century, but Leon claimed more: its rulers projected themselves as 'Emperors' over all Iberian states, Christian and Muslim. Leon had indeed taken the lead against Andalus, but its claim to empire sounded increasingly hollow as the 11th century drew to a close. Nevertheless Leon remained a potent force and its military aristocracy became increasingly feudalised. Fiefs became hereditary, though in the 12th century a knight could still pass on his arms, armour and horse to an heir only if he died in action—if he died in bed his gear reverted to the king. Urban militia infantry forces were, however, relatively undeveloped in Leon even by the 13th century.

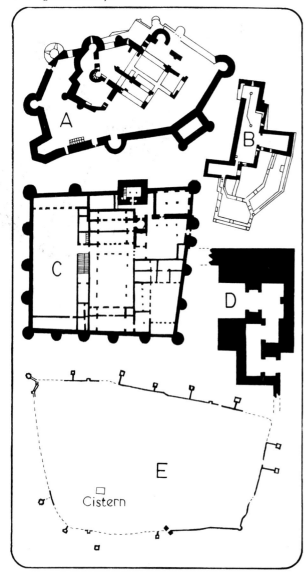

Castile

The military systems of neighbouring Castile were rooted in those of Leon. In the late 11th century a king or baron could give arms to any free man in return for military service, while equipment could also be captured directly from the foe or purchased with the profits of booty. The division of spoils was, in fact, carefully regulated throughout Castile. Different forms of warfare were reflected in summons to service. *Fonsado* or *hueste* were formal expeditions on horseback, while defensive actions against enemy raids were called *apellido*. *Anubda* and *arrobda* entailed siege, pitched battle, frontier guard or garrison work. Failure to answer any such summons led to a fine or *fonsadero*, this eventually evolving into a form of tax with which a ruler could pay professional troops.

From the mid-11th to mid-12th centuries the Castilian army basically consisted of noble *caballeros hidalgos* who fought as vassals in return for fiefs or pay. Many, like the king himself, had their own professional private armies or *mesnadas*. These in turn were led by members of the *infanzones* or lesser nobility such as El Cid. Of increasing importance were non-noble but prosperous *caballeros villanos* who fought in return for tax exemptions. They could, however, lose such status if they failed to attend a twice yearly military inspection properly equipped and mounted. Urban infantry *pedones* also fought in return for privileges. The *juez* or leader of an urban force was usually appointed by the king, but each city section elected its own *alcalde* or leader when it joined a campaign. Other vital militia auxiliaries included the *atalayeros* scouts. They were something of an élite, mounted on the swiftest horses and paid a special salary. Like many Spanish military terms these titles often come from Arabic. During a raid these forces were divided into two parts, one of which built and defended a base camp while the rest, the *algara* or raiders, rode on to do what damage they could. Rules governing a city's involvement in warfare were enshrined in its *fuero* charter; these covered information-gathering, espionage, the division of spoils, compensation for

(A) Almenara castle (Cuenca), late 14th C. around 11th–12th C. core. (B) Calatrava la Nueva (Ciudad Real), early 13th C. castle within 15th C. enlargement. (C) Aljaferiya Palace (Saragossa), 1046–81. (D) Gate of the Law, Alhambra Palace (Granada), 1348. (E) Almohade defences of Caceres, showing *albarrana* towers projecting from the circuit wall, late 12th C.

death or injury, and the exchange of prisoners. Medieval Spain was, as the historian L. Lourie put it, 'a society organised for war'.

As new territory was overrun so new towns had to be created and conquered ones repopulated. At first such colonisation was spontaneous, only later being formalised by the government. For much of the 11th century lands between the Douro River and high sierras were bandit country to which outlaws and escaping serfs fled from both sides. Yet the rôle of urban militias was so important in the Reconquista that Castilian kings eagerly granted new charters, gave new freedoms and encouraged the colonisation of such new territories. The sierras then remained a battle zone between Christendom and Islam until, with the fall of Toledo in the late 11th century, the frontier was again pushed south, away from the mountains and onto the high plains of New Castile. Raiding now took a new turn with large-scale cattle rustling virtually being invented in 12th century Toledo. Desire for the rich winter grazing lands of La Mancha also played its part in a frontier society for whom cattle represented an obvious form of wealth. Such a military system was highly effective when facing fragmented Muslim city states with comparable militias. It failed, however, against united foes like the Almoravids and Almohades.

Aragon

Military developments differed in Aragon. Men from southern France played a significant rôle in the reconquest and colonisation of eastern Spain, though official French participation ceased by the mid-12th century. Foreign involvement did not, however, get off to a happy start. The capture of the Muslim frontier town of Barbastro in 1064 was largely the work of Norman, French and Italian Crusaders who broke the surrender terms and slaughtered not only the defenders but also some 6,000 male inhabitants whose women and children were then divided among the conquerors as concubines or slaves. Thousands more were sent to the Byzantine Emperor as a gift and only a year later Barbastro was retaken by the Andalusian rulers of Saragossa.

Saragossa was itself the key to north-eastern Andalus and its seizure by Alfonso I of Aragon in 1118 opened the entire region to gradual conquest.

'Soldiers at the Holy Sepulchre', wall painting from San Baudelio de Berlanga, Soria. Unlike other pictures from the same hermitage, this is in purely Romanesque style. The soldiers' helmets have particularly broad nasals, they have mail ventails across their faces and carry extremely large shields. (Museum of Fine Arts, Boston)

Its fall followed a long hard siege against a garrison with 20 mangonels plus an even more determined citizen militia. Many starved before surrendering and even then the survivors only capitulated after the defeat of an Almoravid relief force. Unlike events at Barbastro, the Muslim inhabitants of Saragossa were given a suburb in which to live and, what is more, these terms were kept though most Saragossans still preferred to leave for Muslim-held territory. Alfonso I of Aragon, 'The Battler' as he came to be known, died after falling into an ambush while raiding Muslim Lerida in 1134.

Catalonia

Catalonia and Aragon were to unite under one crown and become the second biggest power in Spain; but Catalonia's culture, as the easternmost Iberian state, was different from those of other Christian kingdoms. Effectively unified under Count Berenguer I in 1064, its name like that of Castile originally meant land of castles, or more accurately of castle-holders. This was a region of numerous small and often poor fiefs. Military obligation was based on personal fidelity and property rather than true feudalism, though after

1200 concepts of vassalage did develop under strong French influence. Nevertheless Catalan military obligation remained confused and unclear, the great vassals of Barcelona clearly owing the count some military duties while in other areas service seems to have been purely voluntary.

Portugal

Portugal, as the westernmost state in Christian Iberia, also differed from the general pattern. It was not, in fact, fully recognised as a separate entity by the others until the 13th century, and much of Portugal's effort went into preserving its independence from Leon and Castile. The country's military organisation was old-fashioned, or at least remained true to an Arab-Andalusian tradition, until the 14th century. The army commander had an Arabic title, *alferes mor*, as did the *alcalde* governors of castles or fortified cities. Portuguese costume continued to be influenced by Mozarab-Andalusian styles while an even older tradition may have lain behind a continued use of longbows, though crossbows had also come into fashion.

Taifa and Almoravid Armies

When Muslim Andalus settled down after the collapse of the Caliphate of Cordova a kaleidoscope of petty states emerged, some quite large, others consisting of little more than one town. These have too often been dismissed as self-defeating, as inviting destruction by the growing power of Christian Iberia, and as surrendering to an African-Islamic Empire as the only means of prolonging the existence of Andalusian Islam. Such a view is, however, oversimplified.

These *taifa* (party or group) states represent an example of the Iberian tradition of regionalism, a tradition directly opposed to a centralising concept of unification. Both still exist and can still be seen in Spain. The *taifas* were also part of a wider trend in 11th century Islamic history and were mirrored by events in Iran where another people, similarly conquered by Arabs in the early Islamic period,

Wall painting from San Baudelio de Berlanga, Soria early 12th C. In this Mozarab style painting a huntsman uses a large crossbow of primitive construction. (Prado Museum, Madrid)

reasserted their identity. Iran's revival remained within the Islamic orbit; but in Iberia Christians were numerous, perhaps even an overall majority, while neighbouring Christian states could draw upon the growing strength of Europe beyond the Pyrenees. Most significant of all, perhaps, was the fact that the Muslims did not appreciate the changes taking place to their north. They were confident of cultural superiority and were accustomed to military security. It simply did not occur to *taifa* rulers that the despised Christians of northern Iberia posed a serious threat—not, at least, until it was almost too late. And why should they? Crusades to the Holy Land had yet to begin, and everywhere else except Sicily, Islam was victorious.

Taifa states also differed from one another. The biggest, Badajoz, Toledo and Saragossa, were centred upon the *thughur* or military frontier zones of the old Caliphate. The tiniest were clustered in the south-west (*al Gharb* or the Algarve) far from the Christian frontier, while some were ruled by an Andalusian aristocracy which thus enjoyed power for the first time in a century.

Comparable fragmentation was taking place in North Africa; in fact Ceuta and Tangier, at the very northern tip of Morocco, formed a *taifa* state, having previously been part of the Andalusian Caliphate. From *c*.1060 to the 1070s Ceuta was ruled by Barghawata Berbers, a people who, having evolved their own peculiar religion, were considered infidel by ordinary Muslims. Though powerful enough to field 12,000 horsemen, the

'Army and Court of Nebuchadnezzar', *Beatus of Liebana*, c.1220. These figures are probably based upon Andalusian warriors. Their equipment is essentially similar to that of Christian Spain except for large round shields having decorative tassels such as those seen on later *adarga* shields. (Ms. 429, Pierpont Morgan Lib., New York)

Carved portal showing a warrior with a rigid face-covering visor on his helmet and a large kite-shaped shield, *c.*1155 (*in situ* Santa Maria la Real, Sanguessa, Navarre).

parently hoping to reunite Andalus under its own rule. Others, like Saragossa, allied themselves with their Christian neighbours, getting some assistance in return. Warfare was not, in fact, a normal way of settling disputes among the *taifa* states and when faced by Christian threats they paid tribute, made pacts and encouraged inter-Christian rivalries. Some *taifa* states, including Seville, retaliated with raids, albeit rare and often unsuccessful ones.

None the less the *taifa* states did have warrior élites though there was less class differentiation than in the Christian north, family or tribal ties being more important. Military tenancies, often centred around small castles, were increasingly hereditary, while garrisons were paid as well as owing semi-feudal obligations to the local *qa'id* governor or castle-holder. Towns were a more important source of military strength. These were similarly dominated by great families, as is the case in much of the Middle East today, while even the Mozarab Christian nobility seems to have risen in military importance. Though the role of infantry increased as Islam went on the defensive, the most prestigious soldiers were still cavalry. These followed a code of conduct similar to the 'knightly' ideals of their Spanish counter-parts. Their skills, organisation and equipment of mail and quilted armour, long swords and spears, heavy shields and helmets, were clearly comparable. Face-covering mail coifs are mentioned, as are leather *lamt* shields imported from the Sahara, while crossbows were now the most important infantry weapon.

The Almoravids 1085–1250

The *Murabitin*, or Almoravids as they were known in Spain, originated as a fundamentalist Islamic sect among the Afro-Berbers of the western Sahara shortly before 1050. As inhabitants of the deep desert they owned few horses and fought almost entirely as infantry, though combat on camel-back was also recorded. Later Almoravids reportedly had 30,000 thoroughbred camels, saddled and ready for war. At first, however, they adopted phalanx formations in which a front rank knelt behind long spears and tall shields of tanned oryx skin while rear ranks threw javelins. Later Almoravid cavalry also used long, almost body-covering shields. Such tactics were essentially static, supposedly never retreating nor even pursuing a

Barghawata were eventually crushed by the Almoravids after a fierce struggle, Ceuta falling in 1078/9. This left the fierce Saharan Almoravids poised on the Straits of Gibraltar. Elsewhere in North Africa a Fatimid withdrawal to Egypt and an invasion by nomad Beni Hilal tribes added to the confusion.

The fall of Toledo to the Castilians and of Valencia to El Cid sent shock waves throughout the Muslim west. But what could be done? The *taifa* states were neither strong nor particularly rich; some had armies of only a hundred or so men. A few employed North African or Christian Spanish mercenaries, Seville being one. But Seville was more aggressive and expansionist than the rest, ap-

defeated foe. A minority wore mail hauberks, and all relied on curved daggers for close combat.

The name *Murabitin* probably reflected this immobility and formation, rather than the *ribat* or fortress with which it is often associated. Traditional Berber and Saharan tactics had long relied on a barricade or laager of camels from which tribesmen launched repeated charges. Like nomad tactics everywhere, this avoided undue casualties among a scarce manpower. The dedicated Almoravids, however, accepted heavy losses, and thus for years proved virtually invincible, particularly after they had won allies among richer north Saharan cavalry tribes. The role of such horsemen was now to break and pursue a weakened foe, which in turn added flexibility to Almoravid tactics. From the earliest days flags played a leading part in battlefield control, again perhaps reflecting greater discipline compared to other North African armies. Although the first Almoravid leader regarded war-drums as pagan devices, later Almoravid forces made great use of them, particularly in Iberia where they terrified the Christians and panicked their horses. The most characteristic feature of the Almoravid warrior was, however, his *litham* or face veil. The Almoravids were said to regard the mouth as unclean and to refer to unveiled peoples as 'the fly-mouthed'.

Yusuf ibn Tashfin, second Almoravid leader and the man destined to conquer Andalus, reorganised these armies. Original Almoravid forces had been a tribal confederation, but Yusuf changed the command structure and created a personal force of black slaves and foreigners. His bodyguard consisted of 500 non-Berber horsemen, including Arabs, Turks and Europeans, supported by a further 2,000 black African cavalry. Christian mercenaries as well as converted Spanish prisoners continued to fight for the Almoravids and their successors both in Andalus and North Africa throughout the late 11th and 12th centuries.

Cavalry also became more important than camel-mounted troops, particularly when operating in Andalus. There the high number of black Africans in Almoravid armies, many recruited from Senegal on the southern frontier of the empire, had a terrifying effect on Christian morale—as did the use of massed drums, unusual forms of bow, enormously long leather shields, bamboo spears

'Sleeping guard at the Holy Sepulchre', relief carving in Monastery of S. Domingo do Silos, Castile, 1135–40. Here soldiers have mail drawn across their faces and wear peculiar helmets with extensions to protect the neck and what appears to be reinforcements across the crown (from plaster cast in the Victoria & Albert Museum, London).

and other unfamiliar weapons. A continuing use of large numbers of camels also unsettled the Spaniards' horses although, in fact, such animals had been known in southern Andalus since at least the 10th century. Above all the Spaniards were completely out-manoeuvred by the highly mobile Almoravids, leading them to believe that their foes were much more numerous than they really were. Even in Iberia, however, the Almoravids ultimately relied on an infantry phalanx which now also served as a safe haven from which cavalry could emerge and to which they would return. This was not, of course, a new tactic, but it had been refined by the Almoravids who also gave their horsemen greater freedom of action. Yet the élite status of mounted troops should not be overemphasised as there are reports of men riding mules in battle when horses were unavailable.

(A) 'Massacre of the Innocents', (B) 'Guards of King Herod', carved facade late 12th C. The mailed warriors are identical to those of France except for their very long tunics, while Herod's unarmoured men carry a sword, a long-bladed weapon on a short haft and a curved weapon with an additional spike. All perhaps reflect the similarity between Christian and Muslim troops in Iberia (*in situ* S. Domingo, Soria).

introduced, to be rapidly copied by the Christians. The Muslim frontier was strengthened, being defended by local militias and religious volunteers backed up by Almoravid units. Strategic cities like Cacares were garrisoned by what can only be described as Muslim 'monk-soldiers'. Such men, in a long-established Islamic tradition, dedicated part of their lives to these duties before returning to their families.

Christian Armies 1150-1300

The late 12th and 13th centuries were culturally rich for the Christian kingdoms of Iberia. But it was a warlike era, not only between two faiths but also between Christian states as they squabbled over their spoils. The destruction, depopulation and agricultural decline of huge areas in what had been Muslim Andalus lasted well beyond the Middle Ages. Further south and east much of the Muslim

In Andalus the Almoravids not only checked the Christian advance but rolled it back a short way. They also took over or rendered tributary all the *taifa* states, and strengthened an already growing sense of *jihad*. This concept of Holy War was, however, almost entirely concerned to defend Islam rather than to extend it. On the other hand an atmosphere of *jihad* eroded traditional Andalusian toleration. Such erosion similarly accompanied growing Crusader ideas on the Christian side of the frontier. Persecution of the Andalusian Mozarabs increased and a habit of head-hunting was

and Mozarab peasantry remained, yet a massive exodus by the Andalusian élite left great gaps in the population.

Everywhere the Iberian Military Orders were in the forefront, dealing with such situations. Apart from their military role these Orders had three other vital functions: local government in areas virtually outside royal control, religious control, and the promotion of colonisation. They gave land to secular lords and tried to develop towns. Famous Orders like the Templars and Hospitallers came early on the scene, but tended to regard Iberia as a source of revenue for operations in the Holy Land. Consequently they were driven from Castile and replaced by purely Spanish Orders such as those of Calatrava, Santiago and Alcantara. Hospitallers and Templars played a more enduring role in Aragon, and survived for some time in Portugal until being replaced by national Orders.

Such Orders were not, however, the first military brotherhoods in Iberia. Temporary confraternities had been formed to defend Belchite in 1122 and Monreal del Campo in 1128. Mutual influences between such organisations and Muslim 'brotherhoods' garrisoning *ribats* along the Andalusian frontier also seems likely. Religion still played a vital part in maintaining morale, though both sides were also extraordinarily fond of capturing trophies, enemy flags being a favoured item while the Muslims delighted in capturing church bells to be converted into mosque lamps.

After 1148 the Iberian kingdoms got virtually no help from the rest of Europe, Crusading energies being channelled to the East. The Spaniards were left alone to cope with the problems of their own success. The major problems came after a great military breakthrough following victory over the Almohades at Las Navas to Tolosa in 1212, yet they had begun much earlier. Conquered areas were not, of course, entirely abandoned. The great cities remained, with their sophisticated economic and political traditions. In New Castile new towns with new *fuero* charters sprang up. Here *peones* might still become *caballeros* if they could afford the equipment,

Arch linking one of the *albarrana* towers (right) to the main wall (left) of Talavera: Almohade, late 12th–early 13th C.

while in Old Castile, society became more rigid. After Castile conquered the Andalusian heartland around Cordova, Seville and Murcia, even greater autonomy was given to military colonists. Cities like Cordova, Jaen and Baeza, which were to remain close to a war-torn frontier for another two centuries, established *hermandad* militias and leagues for mutual defence. These served not only against Muslim raids but also in the many Castilian civil wars.

Portugal's drive southward was equally dramatic and had a similarly profound effect on the country's military, cultural and naval future. Again, however, the conquest at first brought problems, up to half of some towns fleeing to Granada or North Africa.

In Aragon and Catalonia, united since 1162, the old semi-feudal structure had been defensive. What was needed now were readily available armies to hold down huge new territories. South of the fertile

‘Cepheus’, *Book of Fixed Stars*, Ceuta, Morocco, 1224. This extremely rare illustrated manuscript from North Africa shows a figure wearing a segmented helmet with a neck extension like a very early bascinet. (Ms. Ross. 1033, Vatican Lib., Rome)

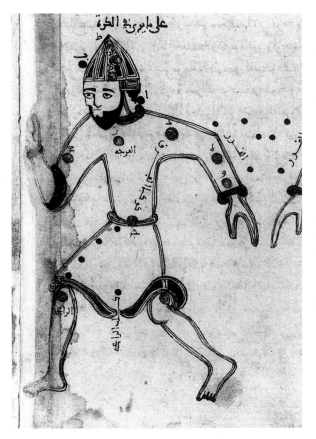

Ebro valley Aragon conquered an arid, sparsely populated and mountainous land. This was divided into military zones settled by peasant infantry and horsemen governed by their own customary laws. The kings still rewarded their followers with lands, of which there were plenty, but royal power was limited while that of a few baronial families grew.

In the deep south, around Valencia, there was little Christian settlement until the Muslim risings of the 1260s. Aragon-Catalonia's defeat in southern France (Albigensian Crusade) and the death of King Peter at the battle of Muret were serious blows to a crown already beset by problems. Peter's successor James came to the throne virtually penniless. His subsequent seizure of Muslim Majorca in an interesting example of combined land-sea operations was a gamble that opened up trade across the western Mediterranean, thus solving many of the king's money problems. The presence of many Catalan mercenary soldiers in North Africa also gave subtle political leverage.

A lack of fully developed feudal attitudes in 13th century Aragon obviously influenced the country's military organisation. Most soldiers were paid professionals. Militias, including fully armed citizen cavalry, were effective, while the cities and church had more real power than the barons. Even the king's influence was largely administrative, while in the Muslim south Aragonese rule over Valencia was little more than a military occupation. The unreliability of the barons made a full-time royal army an obvious necessity. This was now built around the king's small *mesnada* using local, English, French, Italian and even Hungarian mercenaries. It was expensive but a solution was found in taxes that lay under direct crown control, the most significant being that paid by the kingdom's Jewish community. A significant and almost bloodless victory was won by this new army in 1280 when King Peter captured much of the country's nobility by seizing a castle in which they had gathered to plot against him.

But the king of Aragon had to face other troubles as well, above all from Muslims who formed a majority of the southern population. This area at first preserved sufficient independence for a large part of the Andalusian élite to remain. A local Christian Mozarab nobility had also played an interesting rôle even before the Aragonese conquest.

In the 1160s, for example, the Azagra family held some mountain valleys, first as vassals of Muslim Valencia and then as independent rulers. After the fall of Valencia the Azagras extended their territory until the family died out in 1276. Muslim *qa'ids* also survived the conquest, administering a Muslim countryside and supplying the king with troops. Among these lords was a certain al Azraq who, in 1244, did homage for eight castles around a small palace in the Alcala valley. Al Azraq and his fellow *mudejar* ('tamed') Muslim lords might have continued in relative freedom if circumstances had not pushed them into revolt. Increasing Christian colonisation might have been the major cause, and it was certainly a serious affair. Trouble began in 1245 but really exploded two years later. The rebels retreated into al Azraq's mountains where they seized more castles and maintained a guerrilla war, crushing a major Christian offensive around 1249 and almost capturing King James. The next few years saw stalemate while the Aragonese faced further defeat in southern France. Fighting then flared up in 1256, and two years later, following agreement with Castile, King James launched an all-out assault, seized al Azraq's main citadel and brought the rebels to heel. Even these events did not end Andalusian participation in Christian armies— Valencian Muslims fought for Aragon against a French invasion only a few years later.

The role of Iberian urban militias continued, however, to be more important, particularly in Castile. Such troops were present at the great victory of Las Navas de Tolosa, in the capture of Cordova in 1236, Valencia in 1238 and Seville in 1248. Militias along the frontier were also strengthened and reorganised in the late 12th and 13th centuries. Regulations concerning equipment became more specific: horses had to be of a minimum quality, *caballeros* had to have shields, lances, metal helmets, swords, mail hauberks and padded *perpunt* soft-armours plus arm and thigh defences. Certain troops such as standard-bearers

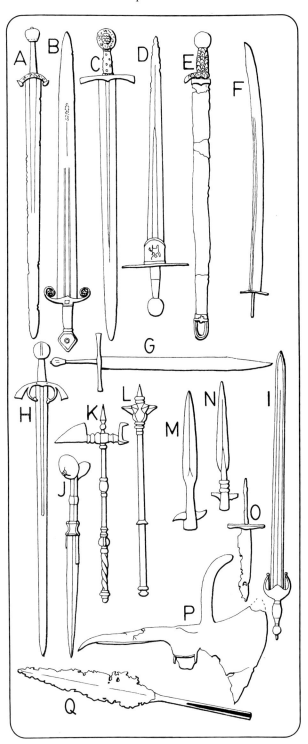

Iberian weapons. (A) Sword, 11th–13th C. (Alava Prov. Museum, Vitoria). (B) 'Sword of St. Ferdinand', prob. Andalusian blade 13th C. (Real Armeria, Madrid). (C) Sword 13th C. (Instituto Valencia Don Juan, Madrid). (D) 'Sword of St. Martin', Aragonese? *c.*1300 (Musée de l'Armée, Paris). (E) Sword from St. Martin's Cave, Gibraltar, Andalusian? early 14th C. (British Museum, London). (F) Blade called 'Gajere', North African or Mamluk with shortened modern hilt (regalia of Katsina emirate, Nigeria). (G) Falchion from Puente Genil. *c.*1350–1400 (Archaeol. Museum, Cordova). (H) Sword *c.*1500 (Instituto Valencia Don Juan, Madrid). (I) *Jinete* sword from Granada, late 14th C. (Met. Mus. of Art, New York). (J) Ear-dagger, prob. from Granada late 14th–early 15th C. (Instituto Valencia Don Juan, Madrid). (K–L) Maces, 15th C. (Army Museum, Madrid). (M–N) Spearheads, 12th–14th C. (Alava Prov. Museum, Vitoria). (O) Dagger, Andalusian? 12th–14th C. (S. Juan Duero Museum, Soria). (P) Axe-head, 13th–14th C. (Alava Prov. Museum, Vitoria). (Q) Spearhead, 10th–13th C. (Nat. Archaeol. Mus., Madrid).

Torre de Oro, Seville: Almohade 1220. Though now standing alone, this structure once formed a very large *albarrana* tower linked to the main ramparts. Its third level is an 18th C. addition.

important were the herdsmen that they were exempt from other military duties. The oldest descriptions of an escort system date from the late 12th century. According to these, the herds were gathered under an *esculca* or *rafala* guard consisting of one *caballero* for each herd of cattle, one for each three flocks of sheep. A leader or *alcalde* was elected by the *esculqueros* before the *pastores* (shepherds) and *vaqueros* (cowboys) drove their animals south. The entire outfit returned in March, the *esculca* being disbanded before the animals set off again. This time they headed north into the high sierras with a smaller infantry escort.

This ranching system had a profound impact on Castilian military developments. By the end of the 13th century the overall command structure was being modernised, as were tactics. Alfonso X, called the 'Learned', advocated a cone formation for armoured cavalry that was almost certainly based on a Byzantine original, probably via Arabic military manuals. Armour and weapons grew heavier, horse armour was common, soft armour was worn over rather than under mail, and a greater use of scale armour reflected the threat from crossbows. Hardened leather armour for the limbs and coats-of-plates for the body were increasingly popular, but all-enveloping great helms and heavy iron plate armour never became as widespread as in neighbouring France. This presumably reflected climatic as much as tactical considerations. Islamic influence could still be seen in helmet decoration. The mace was perhaps more of a symbol of rank than a real weapon, while in Iberia the sword and its hilt were widely regarded as a symbol of the Cross. Paradoxically some surviving examples are decorated not only with Islamic arabesque designs but even with Koranic quotations translated into Latin. It has also been suggested that a Spanish type of single-edged falchion with an angled back showed Eastern influence via Islamic Andalus. This weapon was certainly popular and has survived into modern times as the machete.

The distinction between armoured and light horsemen, both in their tactical rôles and equipment, was becoming more distinct. The importance of infantry was yet to decline, despite the fact that some peasant auxiliaries were armed with primitive slings as late as the mid-14th century. Javelin-armed mountaineers from Navarre and the Basque

must also have horse-armour. Other regulations dealt with the weaponry of infantry and mounted crossbowmen.

Some militias were now involved in the protection of great herds that migrated to and from seasonal pastures in central Spain. Until the Muslims were driven into their last mountain fastness around Granada they too had used these grasslands, much of their terminology being adopted by the Spaniards. Both sides raided each other's herds; and there was also competition between southern and northern Castilian cities, animals representing many a city's wealth. While the high sierras provided summer grazing, the rich southern grasslands were vital as winter pasture. So

country were in wide demand as mercenaries well into the 14th century while Catalonia was famous not only for the manufacture of crossbows but also for its crossbowmen.

Aragon, however, was also the homeland of a distinctive warrior—the *almugavar*. His name again comes from Arabic (*al mughawir*—raiders) and he formed the professional backbone of 13th and 14th century Aragonese armies. Some *almugavars* were cavalry but most fought on foot. All were lightly armed with swords, javelins or crossbows and wore forms of leather armour. Many were of 'Moorish' origin and some may still have been Muslim. They formed the bulk of the famous Catalan Grand Company, a mercenary unit that rampaged across Greece and Anatolia early in the 14th century, where their background probably accounted for their ability to get on so well with Muslim Turks. At home their guerrilla tactics broke the back of a French invasion early in the 13th century and they also served in Aragon's growing empire in Sicily, Sardinia and elsewhere. A peasant militia or *sometent* was similarly raised in many parts of Aragon-Catalonia to maintain the king's 'Peace and Truce', while various cities, including those of Catalonia, developed new militias called *hermandades* to police an increasingly turbulent age.

Almohades and Andalusians 1120-1270

The *Muwahhidun*, or Almohades as they were known in Spain, originated as a reformist Islamic sect in the mountains of Morocco. Unlike the nomadic Afro-Berber Almoravids, whom they overthrew, the Almohades were strictly Berber and evolved in a partially urbanised region. Their military structure was consequently quite sophisticated from an early stage. The Almohade army was, however, still organised on a tribal basis though it soon included black slaves and Almoravid deserters. The blacks included *itabbalan* drummers responsible for huge kettledrums. In fact, the Almohades made even greater use of war-drums than had their predecessors, the biggest being several yards in circumference with its skin

'Massacre of the Innocents', with a rare carving of a flat-topped great helm and short-sleeved surcoat, late 13th C. (*in situ* Santa Maria la Real, Olite, Navarre)

stretched over a gold and green wooden case. Other élite troops included archers of Ghuzz Turkish origin.

Though Almohade tactics were similar to those of the early Almoravids, a description by one warrior indicates significant differences. He wrote:

'We formed a square in the flat land. On all four sides we placed a rank of men with long spears in their hands. Behind them stood a second line with spears and javelins while behind them were men with bags of stones (slingers). Behind all stood archers while the cavalry were in the middle of the square. Whenever the Almoravid horsemen charged towards us they met only the long-bladed spears, the javelins, the stones and the arrows. Some died in the charge and others turned to flee but then the Almohade cavalry charged through lanes which the infantrymen made in their ranks, striking upon the enemy's wounded or fallen. If the Almoravids attacked again then they (the Almohade horsemen) withdrew within the forest of spearblades.'

**Fortified church of S. Juan, Puertomarin, Galicia, early 13th C.
Such churches acted as places of refuge in troubled times.**

Such tactics were refined still further in Andalus and at the decisive but close-run battle of Las Navas de Tolosa the Almohades reinforced their field defences with a chained palisade. This entered the mythology of the Reconquista as chains with which the Almohade ruler's guards were supposedly fastened together.

Another characteristic feature of the purely Berber warrior was an ancient habit of shaving his head before battle. The growing isolation of these western lands from the Arab Middle East started in the 11th century and led not only to the disappearance of Arab costume but also to a period of Berberisation in Andalusian styles. The puritanical Almohades were not, however, well received in Andalus, where rich costume was still preferred by those who could afford it, including the military élite. Almohade rule also seems to have been deeply unpopular and was largely maintained by force.

As the Christian conquest pressed south, so more and more areas were treated as frontier zones. These military regions were governed by a *wali* and each city had a governor or *qa'id* with an average standing garrison of around 100 men. Following defeat at Las Navas de Tolosa in 1212, the spell of Almohade power was broken and local rulers reasserted their independence in many parts of Andalus. This was to be the third and final *taifa* period.

The second had lasted for only a few years between the collapse of the Almoravids and the coming of the Almohades. Yet in both these later *taifa* periods small local armies emerged, well trained and determined to preserve an Andalusian identity. One of the most interesting revivals of the second *taifa* period occurred in the west, in what is now southern Portugal. Here a mystic named Ibn Qasi declared himself to be the Mahdi (the right-guided one who would purify Islam), won a considerable following, captured a series of castles in 1144 and almost seized Seville. After various ups and downs Ibn Qasi appealed to the Portuguese for help, and was consequently assassinated by his own men. During this same chaotic period Lisbon fell to a combined force of English Crusaders and Portuguese.

In Castile the advancing Christians treated the native Andalusians with respect while slaughtering Almoravids. They even sent the son of the last independent king of Saragossa, Sayf al Dawla, south in an attempt to raise a general revolt against the Almoravids. Sayf al Dawla had, in fact, held lands around Toledo as a vassal of the Castilian crown ever since the Almoravids drove his family from Saragossa, but his attempt to set up a vassal Andalusian state was short-lived. Thrown out of Cordova and Granada, Sayf al Dawla went on to take Murcia and Valencia in 1146 but was killed in a quarrel with his own Castilian soldiers. The area then fell to a certain Ibn Mardanish, known to the Spaniards as 'King Lobo', who hated the North Africans more than he did the Christians. Though a Muslim, Ibn Mardanish spoke Spanish, dressed in Spanish style, used Spanish troops and military equipment, and even recruited mercenaries from Italy. He formed an alliance with Castile and resisted the Almohades until his death. In fact Ibn Mardanish, together with the Military Orders and the Portuguese, put up the only effective resistance to the Almohades. Eventually, however, he was besieged in Murcia whereupon his Christian allies turned against him. Betrayed and broken-hearted, 'King Lobo' died in 1172, instructing his son to hand Murcia over to his life-long foes the Almohades.

The rise of petty rulers following the Almohade decline involved civil wars that made the Christian advance much easier, and this time there was no North African empire ready to reimpose Muslim central rule. Instead the Andalusian nobility squabbled over a mosaic of castle-kingdoms while attempting to come to terms with the advancing Christians. Local forces may have been dedicated and well trained, but they were few. Only those nearest the frontier put up much resistance, and once they had been defeated the whole of Andalus lay open to conquest.

In many ways Andalusian warriors were now virtually identical to their Christian counterparts, with a comparable code of chivalry and a delight in the single combat of champions. It was quite common for Christian leaders to dub members of Andalusian embassies as knights. Their arms and armour were almost the same, with long heavy lances, heavy shields hung on guiges, full mail coifs and perhaps even face-covering helmets. Horse-armour was now common among Andalusian cavalry, though rare in North Africa. Andalusian horsemen also used tall saddles, a straight-legged riding position and the couched lance. Occasional great victories, like that at Ecija in 1275, made huge

quantities of Spanish equipment available, though such arms and armour are likely to have found more favour among Andalusians than their North African allies. Even Andalusian costume showed increasing Spanish influence, while Andalusian infantry were now more important than ever, being famed as crossbowmen using heavy and lighter forms of this weapon on both land and sea.

Out of such confusion one strong state emerged: the kingdom of Granada. The area's population had naturally increased as refugees fled before the Christian advance. Many of the newcomers were warriors, eager for revenge and determined to preserve this last bastion of Iberian Islam. Yet this did not stop such troops from being sent to serve Castilian kings, for the Nasrid dynasty which ruled Granada had also been vassals of Castile ever since 1246. Christian troops from the north, perhaps political exiles, similarly served the king of Granada as bodyguards while others fought alongside Andalusian mercenaries in Morocco.

In North Africa another powerful dynasty had emerged from the Almohade wreck. These were the Marinids of Morocco, who also became involved in Iberian affairs; unlike their predecessors, however, the Berber Marinids were never powerful enough to conquer what was left of Andalus nor to drive back the Christian Reconquista. Militarily their tactics

Effigy of Don Alvaro de Cabrera the Younger from Bellpuig, early 14th C. This Catalan nobleman is shown wearing a rigid bevor around his throat, probably a coat-of-plates with sleeves, greaves and scale-lined sabatons on his feet. (Cloisters Museum, New York)

were traditional, being much the same as those of the Almohades, although the importance of infantry seems to have declined. Marinid cavalry were lightly equipped, fought with leather *adarga* shields, little body armour and relatively short swords. Their low saddles were much like the modern riding saddle. In the very north of Morocco the port of Ceuta had a special role in the survival of Granada. Not only was it a base for privateers, but its defences were virtually impregnable before the days of gunpowder. Ceuta was, in fact, the key to naval communications between North Africa and Granada, and while its fleet remained powerful, Berber recruits and even whole armies could rapidly be shipped to Andalus.

14th Century
Christian Armies

The 14th century saw a further divergence from mainstream western European styles in the military equipment of Christian Iberia. There was, for example, very little plate armour in early 14th century Spain, whereas lighter equipment such as the coat-of-plates and scale-lined *jacque* were popular. So were heavy *gorgets* to protect the throat, their popularity resulting from dislike of the even heavier great helm and visored bascinet. Further development of the open war-hat led to the typical Spanish *cabacete*. Many helmets were highly decorated or covered with cloth. Such styles resulted from Islamic influence and, more significantly, from the special character of Iberian warfare where light cavalry and crossbows used both on foot and on horseback, were particularly prominent. Highly developed leather defences, including helmets, armour for the body or limbs, horse armour and kidney-shaped *adarga* shields of Moroccan origin, reflected all these factors.

On the other hand military organisation was considered archaic by outside observers. At Najera in 1367 the defeated Castilian army of Henry of Trastamar consisted of armoured knights, few with horse-armour and all being loath to fight on foot, supported by an ill-trained militia of crossbowmen, spearmen, javelin-throwers and slingers. *Jinete* light cavalry, including troops from Granada, fought on the flanks. Given the good record of Iberian soldiers against other northern invasions the catastrophe at Najera probably resulted from a mistaken decision to face their heavier foes in open battle.

Troops from Granada were, in fact, a common feature in late 13th and 14th century Castile. They were effective not only as allies but as foes during the endemic raiding of the Granadan frontier—so much so that Castile, and almost all other Iberian states, developed their own *jinete* light cavalry. The typical equipment of such troops originally consisted of a light steel helmet, leather shield, padded armour, light sword and two short spears or javelins. Some metal armour was added later, but never much. Even their name, *jinete*, was a corruption of Zenata, the Berber tribe which sent many warriors to fight for Granada during this period. Castilian heavy cavalry also shortened their lances, perhaps as a result of *jinete* influence.

Puerto del Sol, Toledo early 14th C. Though built for the Hospitallers this gate of stone and brick is in purely Islamic (Mudejar) style.

1: El Cid, c.1050
2: Alvar Fañez Minaya, c.1075
3: Andalusian *alguazil*, c.1080

A

1: Almoravid drummer, early 12th C.

2: Ahmad Sayf al Dawla, c.1135

3: Christian mercenary, mid-12th C.

B

1: Andalusian lady, mid-13th C.
2: Leonese knight, early 13th C.
3: Almohade footsoldier, early 13th C.

C

1: An average knight, late 13th Century

2: Castilian crossbowman, c.1300

3: Andalusian nobleman, c.1290

D

1: Portuguese knight, c.1350
2: Navarrese footsoldier, mid-14th C.
3: Aragonese knight, c.1325

E

1: Grenadine mounted crossbowman, mid-14th C.
2: Grenadine *qadi*, late 14th C.
3: Grenadine light horseman, mid-14th C.

F

1: Aragonese light horseman, 1445
2: Castilian peasant levy, 1445
3: Don Alvaro de Luna, 1445

G

1: Grenadine footsoldier, late 15th C.
2: Grenadine urban militiaman, late 15th C.
3: Spanish hand-gunner, late 15th C.

H

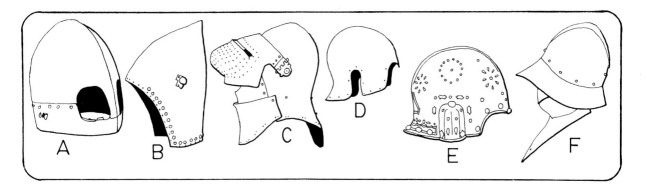

Mobilisation systems differed along various parts of the Castilian frontier with Granada, involving the Military Orders as well as local barons and large numbers of militia cavalry. Frontier lords or *alcades* were often described as being 'between the Christians and Moors', and had as their primary responsibility the maintenance of peace. Beneath them came the *fieles del rastro* or *ballesteros de monte* whose duty was to track down unofficial raiders. Next came the *caballeros de la sierra* who were frontier guards, and the *alfaqueques*, often Jews, who acted as go-betweens whenever problems arose. A large Muslim community survived on the Christian side and this also acted as intermediaries when negotiating the release of prisoners, who were often given into the custody of mosques. Despite such useful roles, the Jewish and Muslim minorities faced increasing hostility by the late 14th century.

In late 14th–15th century Aragon-Catalonia the situation was somewhat different. A temporary division of the country into the kingdoms of Catalonia-Aragon and Rousillon-Majorca ended in 1345 but the Aragonese Mediterranean empire was now in decline. Finances were again low and it was difficult to pay the troops. Urban militias and the *sometent* were perhaps more important than ever. The *almugavers* no longer fought only for the Crown but helped rebels as well. Cross-border marriage alliances meant that many Castilian barons now held fiefs in Aragon, and vice-versa, which led to divided loyalties. Certain Aragonese baronial families were again rising in power, one of the most prominent being that of De Luna. Alvaro de Luna was one baron with a foot in each camp; he became

Iberian helmets. (A) Helmet, 12th–early 14th C. (Scollard Coll., Los Angeles). (B) Bascinet, late 14th C. (Provincial Museum, Burgos). (C) Great bascinet from Pamplona Cathedral, c.1430 (Navarre Mus., Pamplona). (D) Sallet, late 15th C. (Musée de l'Armée, Paris). (E) 'Helmet of Boabdil', Italian sallet with Andalusian decoration, late 15th C. (Met. Mus. of Art, New York). (F) Cabacete and barbote, late 15th C. (formerly Pauillac Coll., Paris)

a strong supporter of an Aragonese claimant to the Castilian throne, virtually manipulating the entire situation. He won a great victory on behalf of King John II of Castile at Olmedo in 1445, only to be disgraced and executed eight years later. There was

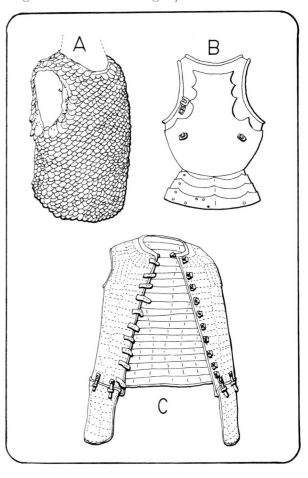

Iberian armour. (A) Cuirass of iron scales, 11th–13th C. (Alava Prov. Museum, Vitoria). (B) 'Cuirass of Duarte de Almeida', 1470–75 (Toledo Cathedral). (C) Brigandine of iron scales under red velvet, 15th C. (Estruch Coll., Barcelona)

'Massacre of the Innocents', carved relief c.1389. The soldiers in this carving are purely Spanish in their equipment, which includes brimmed war-hats, scale-reinforced aventails and plated limb defences. (*in situ* cloisters, Toledo Cathedral)

persistent threat from Castile meant that merchants and artisans were now allowed to keep weapons in their work place, while simple longbows were still used in parts of the country.

Meanwhile the rulers of many Iberian states were increasingly concerned about the way their people dressed, in particular how increasing wealth eroded class differences. Some regulations seem strange to modern ears. In 1340 Alfonso IV of Portugal tried to prevent peasants wearing the tight, leg-revealing hose which had been a mark of the fashionable upper class. Alfonso X of Castile insisted that knights always wear swords and cloaks knotted on the right shoulder, even at meals, and that their clothes be of bright colours such as red, yellow, orange or green; nor should knights ever ride mules.

In the latter half of the 14th century the Hundred Years War spilled south of the Pyrenees, and this had a profound military impact. Northerners had various reasons for getting involved in Iberia. The French wanted to get rid of troublesome mercenaries during a brief spell of peace, while both France and England hoped to improve their strategic positions by winning allies in the south. Individuals were in search of adventure, booty or of eventually fighting the Muslim 'infidels'. The French leader Du Guesclin may even have hoped to carve out his own kingdom in Granada. The military impact was soon seen in a reversion to traditional tactics in Aragon—avoiding a foe when he was on foot and ready, but harassing him when he was mounted and on the march. Here the *jinetes* were in their element. John I of Castile not only reorganised his army along French lines under two senior marshals, but considered reducing its size to a professional core of 4,000 men-at-arms, 1,500 *jinetes* and 1,000 mounted archers or crossbowmen. Meanwhile in Portugal reforms were more fundamental, breaking away from previous Andalusian military structures. The king's vassals had to equip some of their men in English or French style. The role of *alferez mor* was abolished and henceforth military and administrative duties were divided between a *condestabre* (constable) and a *marichal* (marshal) on the English model. The *condestabre* was also given greater disciplinary control over baronial forces, while the old Arabic tactical terms were finally abandoned.

also more external influence upon Aragon than Castile, particularly from Italy, where the Aragonese ruling dynasty maintained a family empire and from which the country imported a great deal of arms and armour.

Navarre, in the far north of Iberia, had lost its frontier with Islam in the early 12th century. Although its armies took part in the fight against Andalus as allies of Castile and Aragon, Navarre was being drawn more and more into the orbit of southern France, from where it imported much military equipment. Small in population but relatively prosperous, Navarre almost always had foreign mercenaries and Muslim troops from the Tudela area in its service. The country's mountainous terrain also led to a greater emphasis on infantry than elsewhere. No major changes were seen in Portugal until the late 14th century. The

The Kingdom of Granada

While there was Islamic influence on Spanish military styles, there was also Spanish influence on aspects of life in Granada. Clothing soon differed from that of North Africa, the rich wearing bright colours while turbans again fell out of fashion. After helping Castile in the battle of Najera the ruler of Granada was even given a coat-of-arms; this was not used on shields or flags but did appear in the architecture of the Alhambra palace in Granada, as well as being incorporated into the decoration of war-drums, weapons and perhaps fabrics.

Frontier towns were strongly fortified under the governorship of a *qa'id*, while Granada itself remained an important arms manufacturing centre. Though there were periods of peace, Granada was aware of the constant Christian threat and evolved tactics to deal with it. These were essentially defensive, though raids were also carried out on Castilian territory. There seems to have been little glamorisation of war, which was described by one writer thus: 'It starts as lamentation, its middle is unpredictable and its end is sorrow.'

Nevertheless, the army was skilled and highly organised; Granada was, for its small size, a significant military power, often able to field more men than its larger foes. A Ministry of War dealt with conscription, payment and administrative matters. Pay varied according to rank and troops included light cavalry, infantry, archers and crossbowmen, many of the latter being mounted. Andalusians formed the *jund* force under *ra'is* and *wali* commanders. The other half of the army consisted of volunteers and exiles from North Africa with a separate command structure under the *shaykh al ghuzat*. An *amir* commanded 5,000 men with a *raya* flag. Under him were the *qa'id* with 1,000 men and an *'alam* flag, the *naqib* with 200 men and a *liwa'* flag, the *'arif* with 40 men and a *band* flag, and the *nazir* with eight men and an *'uqda* lance-pennon. Each soldier also wore a distinctive (but unknown) emblem. Andalusian cavalry had two horses, the spare being led by a squire, whereas North African horsemen had only one mount. Infantry formed a growing majority in these defensive armies, proportions of 3:1 and 6:1 being recorded in 1361. Discipline was strict and reviews were held either weekly, fortnightly or monthly. Training was similarly rigorous for both cavalry and crossbowmen, with special books being written after the manner of the famous Middle Eastern *furusiyya* training manuals. Mosques seem to have played a leading part in the training of urban militias and the storage of their weapons.

Castle of Javier, birthplace of St. Francis Xavier: a fine example of a 14th C. castle with a later church attached.

In the field armies were accompanied by *dalil* guides who knew the mountainous frontier, renegades from Christian ranks, medics, labourers, armourers, poets, orators, plus those religious ascetics who inhabited many frontier towns. According to their enemies such armies were singularly sober, frugal and enduring. There was, however, frequent tension between Andalusians and North African Berbers, particularly the fierce Zenata, and after 1368 Muhammad V of Granada reduced the power of North African troops. His personal guard was now recruited from captive Spanish converts called *ma'lughun* armed with large daggers and other weapons. Such troops of Spanish origin, though never numerous, sometimes rose to high rank. Crossbowmen were, however, probably the most important element in Granadan tactics which relied on harassment, ambush and guerrilla action. In open battle Granadan light cavalry were effective in close combat once heavier Castilian formations had been broken up, but they could rarely face armoured cavalry in a direct charge.

Both sides laid great emphasis on single combat by champions prior to battle or during a siege, while siege warfare itself followed medieval patterns until the widespread introduction of gunpowder.

Profound changes had already taken place in Andalusian-Granadan military equipment during the late 13th and early 14th centuries. Many crossbowmen not only rode to battle but now used their weapons from horseback. Heavy armour, horse-armour and associated tactics using couched lances and a long-legged riding position were abandoned in favour of light cavalry *jinete* styles. Cavalry re-adopted javelins, while lighter swords and fencing styles of sword-play were evolved. Some javelins may even have had feathered flights and the so-called 'ear dagger' was developed, probably from an eastern Islamic prototype, in 14th and 15th century Granada. Some *jinete* swords were especially richly decorated, probably as gifts or bribes for neighbouring Christian aristocrats; many survive to this day. Some late 15th or early 16th century pictorial sources show Granadan troops

Details from a series of carved wooden reliefs illustrating the Conquest of Granada, *c.* 1500 (*in situ* Cathedral Choir, Toledo). (A) Muslim defender of Padul, 1491. (B–C) Spanish hand-gunner and bowman outside unnamed castle. (D) Assault on Alhama 1482. (E) King Ferdinand receives surrender of **Marbella 1485. (F) Spanish *jinete* at surrender of Alora. (G) Ibrahim al Jerbi tries to kill Ferdinand and Isabella outside Guadix 1487. (H) Muslim governor surrenders Setenil. (I) Dismounted Spanish *jinete* at surrender of Vera.**

Painted leather ceiling illustrating an unknown tale, probably painted by a visiting Italian artist, c.1380. Here a Muslim horseman slays a Christian knight. Though totally out of character with other decorations in the Alhambra Palace, two such ceilings show the costume of Granada in great detail (*in situ* Sala de los Reyes, Alhambra, Granada).

using curved sabres. Such weapons may have been introduced from Morocco shortly before the fall of Granada but this is still a debatable question, as are the origins of the curved Moroccan *flyssa*, which was at first a relatively short weapon.

North Africa was, of course, a continuing source of strength for Granada. Muslim Andalusians migrated across the Straits throughout the later Middle Ages. They often fought as mounted or infantry crossbowmen or later as hand-gunners, and did much to help countries like Morocco resist Christian invasion. In fact the guards of 14th century Moroccan rulers included troops from Granada as well as Spanish slaves, Spanish mercenaries and Turkish cavalry. Moroccan equipment was sometimes highly decorated with a lot of gilded metal, red and gilded leather, elaborate saddle-cloths and numerous war-drums. Middle Eastern influence was stronger in Tunisia where maces, light cavalry axes and leather armour were common. Tunisian rulers also had a bodyguard of black slaves from Guinea. Further south in the Sahara and sub-Saharan Sahel regions warriors still

used longbows of simple construction as well as javelins. The cavalry of such Islamic African countries also relied on quilted armour, a little mail and long-hafted spears.

The Fall of Granada

The 15th century saw a re-orientation in Iberian affairs. It began with the early stages of a Portuguese overseas empire, and closed with the discovery of America on behalf of the rulers of Castile and Aragon by Christopher Columbus, just over nine months after the final surrender of Granada.

Before this date, however, both Castile and Aragon endured setbacks. Aragon was wracked by civil war, though its armies became increasingly similar to those of the rest of western Europe. In Castile private war and quixotic duels between nobles were a recurring problem, absorbing more energy than the struggle against the Moors. An extreme case took place in 1434 when Suero de Quiñones and nine other knights held the road to Santiago against all challengers for a month. In this so-called *Passo Honroso* Suero's equipment was carried in a cart driven by a dwarf and preceded by trumpeters, flute players and Moorish drummers. In the more serious warfare of the southern frontier the Duke of Medina Sidonia alone was able to field an army of 4,000 cavalry from his Andalusian estates. A military review covering the Seville area in 1406 listed 142 royal knights, 964 other men-at-arms, 1,276 crossbowmen and 3,720 halberdiers plus 1,904 soldiers from neighbouring villages. Such reviews were held three times a year. The training of the Spanish knight was similar to that of his northern counterparts, but also included mounted bull-fighting which had long been associated with light cavalry skills. His arms and armour may also have seemed exotic to outsiders. Alvaro de Luna, in his account of the battle of Olmedo in 1445, wrote:

'Thus all those noble young gentlemen of the Constable's House ... were very richly adorned. Some had different devices painted on the coverings of their horses, and others jewels from their ladies on their helmet-crests. Others had gold and silver bells, with stout chains hanging to their horses' necks. Others had badges studded with pearls or costly stones around the crests ....

Many different things were put on the helmet crests, for some had insignia of wild beasts, others plumes of various colours, and others had plumes both on their helmet-crests and on the face-coverings of their horses. Some horsemen had feathers that spread like wings against their shoulders ... .'

The similarity between such decorations and those of the Balkans hints at a continuing connection dating back to the 14th century.

The effective unification of Castile and Aragon under King Ferdinand and Queen Isabella meant that for the first time Granada faced a united foe. In fact there had been a considerable increase in Christian aggression before this unification, but the final invasion was more than merely an oversized raid. It was a carefully planned assault designed to extinguish Muslim Iberia once and for all. Ferdinand of Castile was given command of all forces, and his strategy was simply to 'roll up' the kingdom of Granada from all sides, besieging outlying castles and towns before a final attack on the city of Granada. The bulk of Ferdinand's army consisted of paid professionals. Only the great barons now fought as feudal vassals, bringing their own heavy cavalry *lanzas*, more numerous light cavalry *jinetes* and infantry units.

The vital artillery train was attached to the royal forces, which also included many *espingardas* hand-gunners. Other royal troops came from the *Santa Hermandad* or Holy Brotherhood; this was a form of royal conscription established in 1476, paid through local funds but commanded by professionals. Local *hermandad* militia forces from southern Castile

Figures fom an early 14th C. wall painting illustrating warriors using various forms of equipment (*in situ* Torre de las Damas, Alhambra, Granada).

played an important part in the invasion, providing numerous light cavalry and crossbowmen, while other *hermandadas* came from various parts of Castile. So did the strange *homicianos*, condemned criminals offered pardon in exchange for military service. Similar Aragonese contingents used the same weapons and included troops from Sicily, while foreign volunteers also came from England, France, Burgundy, Germany and Flanders.

The campaign was long and bitter, with the Muslims putting up ferocious resistance. When the Christian camp outside Granada was burned down a permanent town called Sante Fé was erected in its place. Even this did not break the defenders' will to resist. In the end the last king of Granada, Boabdil to the Spaniards and Muhammad IX Abu Abdullah to the Muslims, negotiated a private surrender against the wishes of his people, secretly allowing Spanish troops into the Alhambra Palace on 2 January 1492.

'Judges or rulers of Granada', painted leather ceiling, late 14th C. The figures on a third ceiling show men in strictly western Islamic costume, plus swords of the *jinete* type hung from baldrics, (*in situ* Sala de los Reyes, Alhambra, Granada).

Siege, Fortification and Firearms

Some of the Middle Ages' most elaborate defensive systems are to be found in the Iberian peninsula; most are of Islamic origin, though many have magnificent Christian additions. Even before Islam was forced on to the defensive, the frontiers of Andalus were strongly protected by a series of military zones, the *thughur*, where great fortresses served as regional centres of defence. Various materials including stone, brick and a form of concrete were used to strengthen both these and many city walls following dramatic Christian advances in the 11th and 12th centuries. Particular attention was given to adequate water reserves in great cisterns. The Almohades subsequently introduced a sophisticated system of external towers linked to a curtain wall by arched galleries. This probably reflected the adoption of counterweight *trebuchet* stone-throwing machines which, being operated by smaller teams of men, could now be mounted on such towers to provide enfilading fire. Such *albarrana* (Arabic *barrani*—exterior) towers

could, of course, also be occupied by archers or crossbowmen.

The 11th to 13th century Christian states were similarly fortified, though perhaps in a less sophisticated manner. Architects may have been recruited in France and Italy but most castles, walls and gates show the stronger Islamic influence of Andalusian, North African and even advanced Middle Eastern models. Essentially Islamic traditions of bent gates, high walls, rectangular towers and a widespread use of brick persisted right through the 14th century, by which time the influence of France and Italy was perhaps stronger. The situation was similar in Portugal, where most surviving castles are clearly of Andalusian origin with a few later additions such as tower-keeps, chapels and defences against gunfire. Concern for gunpowder artillery first appeared late in the 14th century with the incorporation of gun-emplacements to fire upon a besieger. Only later did military architects feel the need to design defences against firearms.

The last Muslim bastion of Granada was particularly heavily fortified. From the late 13th century its strongly walled frontier towns and castles made use of every natural feature in a mountainous land. Hills overlooking even the most unlikely invasion routes were crowned by small observation posts which also served as places of

Castle of Olmillos de Sasamon, Castile, 15th C. This fortress of the Cartagena family is one of the best preserved of its period but still shows little concern for gunpowder artillery.

refuge from raiders. Meanwhile the long coast was dotted with *tali'a* observation towers, fortresses and heavily defended harbours, all linked by a signal system. The western Islamic states seem, in fact, to have been the first to build regular coastal defences against pirates or invaders. The idea became more common after the 11th century. The name *saracenos* given to the earliest Christian coastal towers in Italy might, in fact, reflect the origin of the idea rather than the expected enemy. The Almohades built such defences in Morocco, but it was the mid-14th century Marinid sultan 'Ali Abu'l Hasan who erected the first complete series of coastal towers on Morocco's Atlantic coast.

Although gunpowder artillery was used in 1359 in the coastal defence of Barcelona and was clearly recorded in Castile by 1362, traditional medieval siege engines were still used during the conquest of Granada over a century later. Fire-weapons comparable to those seen in the Middle East had long been known in Muslim Andalus, but the first record of real gunpowder in this region is more of a problem. Some form of advanced incendiary weapons were used by Muslim forces at Niebla in 1257, in southern Morocco in 1274, at Cordoba in 1280 and at Gibraltar in 1306. Iron balls either propelled by fire or containing fire were used by the forces of Granada against Alicante and Orihuela in 1331. The Marinids and Granadans may have had real artillery in the battles of Salado and Tarifa in 1340, while the Castilians seem to have used the same against Algeciras a few years later. Granada certainly had cannon in 1391.

It was, however, Queen Isabella who really encouraged a widespread adoption of firearms late in the 15th century, bringing in experts from France, Germany and Italy. Firearms made a decisive impact during the conquest of Granada, not only forming part of a royal artillery train of bronze and iron cannon but also in the form of numerous *espingarda* handguns. Of course the Muslims had firearms, including *espingardas* and *ribaudequins*, but they were few in number. These

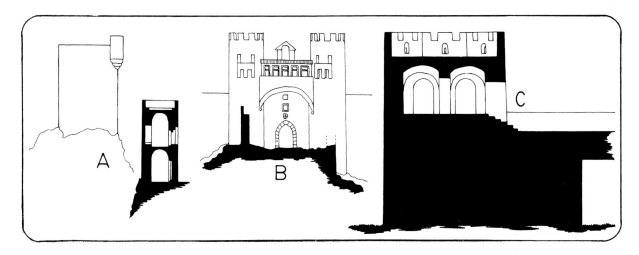

were used at Moclin in 1486 and at Malaga a year later, but only played a significant role in the final struggle for Granada. This city's defences had, in fact, been strengthened with low semi-circular artillery bastions at the base of some high towers. Yet it might still be true to say that, in the end, the last Andalusian kingdom of Granada was betrayed not by its defenders, nor even its last unfortunate king, Boabdil El Zogoiby—'The Unlucky'—but by its lack of modern gunpowder artillery.

Further Reading

R. Arié, *L'Espagne Musulmane au temps des Nasrides (1232–1492)*, Paris 1973.

T. N. Bisson, *The Medieval Crown of Aragon*, Oxford 1986.

R. I. Burns (collected articles), *Moors and Crusaders in Medieval Spain*, London 1978.

A. B. De Hoffmeyer, *Arms and Armour in Spain*, 2 vols, Madrid 1972 & 1982.

(A) Elevation and section of Atienza castle (Guadalahara), mid-12th C. (B) Gate of Siguenza castle (Guadalahara), 1124. (C) Section of Torre Redonda, one of the *albarrana* towers of Caceres, late 12th C.

J. N. Hillgarth, *The Spanish Kingdoms 1250–1516*, 2 vols, Oxford 1976 & 1978.

Ibn Hudhayl, trans. L. Mercier, *La Parure des Cavaliers et l'Insigne des Preux*, Paris 1922.

M. A. Ladero Quesada, *Castilla y la Conquista del Reino de Granada*, Valladolid 1967.

J. D. Latham (collected articles), *From Muslim Spain to Barbary*, London 1986.

D. W. Lomax, *The Reconquest of Spain*, London 1978.

R. Menéndez Pidal, *The Cid and his Spain*, London 1971.

P. E. Russell, *The English Intervention in Spain and*

Iberian firearms. (A) *Trom* with burst muzzle, late 14th C. (Milit. Mus., Lisbon). (B) Iron handgun, 14th C. (unknown locat., Lisbon). (C) Cannon from Baza, 15th C. (Army Mus., Madrid). (D) Handgun with wooden stock, early 15th C. (Armeria Reale, Madrid). (E) Mortar from Burgos, 15th C. (Army Museum, Madrid).

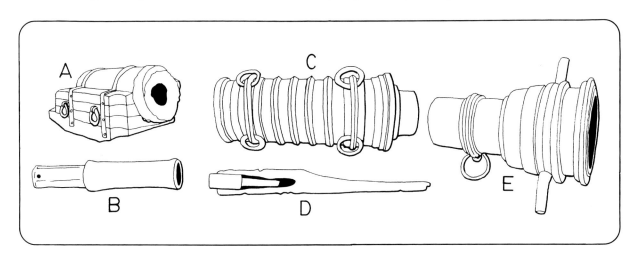

Portugal in the Time of Edward III and Richard II, Oxford 1955.

Al Turtushi, trans. M. Alarcón, *Lámpara de los Príncipes*, Madrid 1931.

D. Wasserstein, *The Rise and Fall of the Party Kings*, Princeton 1985.

These journals also include useful material:
Al Andalus; *Boletin de la Real Academiu de la IIistoria*; *Cuadernos de Historia de España*; *Gladius*; *Hespéris*; *Hispania*; *Le Moyen Age*; *Speculum*.

The Plates

A: El Cid and his times:
A1: El Cid, c.1050
The Spanish hero is here shown in the traditional light equipment used in many parts of 11th century Christian Iberia. Such styles were already giving way before French military influence but would never entirely disappear. El Cid's round shield, relatively light sword and even his red cloak were features also seen on the Muslim side of the frontier. (Sources: sword, Archaeol. Museum, Vitoria; *Beatus Commentaries* 1091–1109, Add. Ms. 11695, Brit. Lib., London; *Liber Testamentorum Regium* early 12th C., Cathedral Lib., Oviedo; 'St. Martin' painted altar front from Puigbó, Dioc. Museum, Vich.)

A2: Alvar Fañez Minaya, c.1075
El Cid's friend uses heavier mail armour and a kite-shaped shield in Catalan style similar to that of southern France. His helmet is of a two-piece construction probably descended from a late Roman prototype, while his sword betrays Islamic influence via Andalusia. The mail flap on his chest is seen in two Catalan manuscripts and recalls a similar feature on the Bayeux Tapestry. Here it is interpreted as an unlaced form of primitive ventail to protect the face. (Sources: *Farfa Bible* 11th C., Vatican Lib., Cod. Lat. 5729, Rome; *Roda Bible* 11th C., Bib. Nat., Ms. Lat. 6, Paris.)

A3: Andalusian alguazil c.1080
Muslim Andalusian troops used equipment reflecting various traditions from the early Islamic Middle East, North Africa, Iberia itself and even Christian Europe. Documentary sources often mention armour but this rarely appears in pictorial sources. Here a middle-ranking officer has a cloak similar to that of El Cid. He is comparatively lightly armed except for a scale-covered cuirass. One such armour survives but its dating is controversial. His light axe clearly betrays eastern influence. (Sources: scale cuirass 11th–13th C., Archaeol. Museum, Vitoria; *Beatus of Facundus* 1047, Bib. Nac., Ms. B.31, Madrid; ivory box from Cuenca 1026, Archaeol. Museum, Burgos; *Arca Santa* c.1075, Camera Santa, Oviedo; *Mozarab Missal* 10th–11th C., Acad. de la Historia, Madrid.)

B: The Kingdom of Saragossa, 1100–1200:
B1: Murabit (Almoravid) drummer, early 12th century
Very few surviving pictorial sources can be directly related to *Murabit* warriors. But abundant written descriptions clearly show that their dress was similar to that worn in parts of North Africa and the Sahara until modern times. Even the forms of their weaponry seem to have survived in isolated parts of the south Sahara and Sudan. The most characteristic feature of this figure is, of course, his *litham* or face-veil. (Sources: *Psalter of San Millán de la Cogolla* 11th C., Acad. de la Historia, Madrid; *Pila Andalusian* carved basin 11th C., Archaeol. Museum, Jativa; *Farfa Bible* 11th C., Vatican Lib., Cod. Lat. 5729, Rome; carvings 12th C., *in situ* west front San Domingo, Soria; *Libro de los juegos* late 13th C., Monastery Lib., Ms. T.j.6, Escorial; 'Arrest of Saint Aventinus' carving late 12th C., *in situ* south portal of church, St. Aventin, Haute-Garonne.)

B2: Ahmad Sayf al Dawla, c.1135
Ahmad Sayf al Dawla, the last Muslim king of Saragossa, wears a full mail hauberk of typically European form. Even the habit of pulling a mail ventail up over the nose is seen in other parts of Europe where archery posed a particular threat. The Moorish king's helmet is, however, unlike anything seen outside the Iberian peninsula and is based on a very clear carving at Santo Domingo de Silos. His long shield appears to be of leather and reflects North African styles. (Sources: 'Guards at the Holy Sepulchre' carving 1135–40, *in situ* cloisters, Monastery of Santo Domingo de Silos;

'Retablo de San Jorge', painted altar-back, *c.*1420. (A) The king of Aragon-Catalonia defeating the Moors. (B) Angels arming St. George (Victoria and Albert Museum, London).

Carving 12th C., *in situ* west front of S. Domingo, Soria; *Bible of Sancho of Navarre* 1197, Bib. Munic., Ms. 108, Amiens.)

B3: Christian mercenary, mid-12th century
Christian warriors fought in many Muslim Iberian armies though Saragossa used them relatively rarely. In general Spanish troops carried French-style equipment though remaining lightly armoured compared to their northern neighbours. One very Spanish feature was, however, a series of helmets that protected much of the wearer's face. These predecessors of the great helm (see plate C2) sometimes had an integral extension to the front of the helmet with eye-holes pierced through it. Others, as here, included a fixed visor riveted to the helmet rim. (Sources: spearhead 12th–14th C., Archaeol. Museum, Vitoria; carved figures *c.*1155, *in situ* west front of S. Maria la Real, Sanguessa; carved capitals late 12th C., *in situ* cloisters of

Cathedral, Tudela; Mozarab *Beatus Commentaries* early 12th C., Archaeol. Museum, Madrid.)

C: The Fall of Andalus, 1200–50:
C1: Andalusian lady, mid-13th century
Less is known about Andalusian female dress than about male costume, though written and pictorial sources agree that it could be very attractive. On the other hand such accounts may romanticise the subject. This lady is largely based upon a unique illustrated Arab-Andalusian love story. Her crown or *taj* also appears in other sources but its actual method of construction is unknown. (Sources: *Bayad wa Riyad* 13th C., Vat. Lib., Ms. Arab 368, Rome.)

C2: Leonese knight, early 13th century
The armies of Leon seem to have been more feudal than those of Castile, with less reliance on non-noble urban troops. This man uses typical knightly gear though with some interesting features. His lack of mail mittens seems old fashioned but the heavy coat-of-plates worn over his mail hauberk is remarkably advanced and may suggest Islamic or

eastern Mediterranean influence on the development of such body armours. (Sources: *Beatus Commentaries* late 12th–early 13th C., Bib. Nat., Nouv. Acq. Lat. 2290, Paris; *Beatus of Liébana* c.1220, Pierpont Morgan Lib., Ms. 429, New York; *Beatus from San Millan de Cogola* 13th C., Acad. de la Historia, Ms. II & III, Madrid; Sword of Fernando de la Cerda mid-13th C., Monastery of Las Huelgas, Burgos.)

C3: Muwahhid *(Almohade) foot soldier, early 13th century*

More is known about the appearance of *Muwahhid* troops than of the *Murabits*, but even so most pictorial sources date from the very end of the *Muwahhid* period. Their costume was essentially the same as that still worn by the urban and rural peoples of North Africa, rather than that of the nomads. This humble soldier wears a traditional hooded *burnus* over a relatively primitive helmet based on a unique early 13th century manuscript from northern Morocco. His long-hafted single-edged weapon is, in contrast, an Iberian device. (Sources: *Book of Fixed Stars* by al Sufi 1224, Vat. Lib., Ms. Ross. 1033, Rome; *Codex Calixtinus* late 12th C., Cathedral Archive, Santiago de Compostella; 'Roland and Faragut' carved capital late 12th C., *in situ* Palace of the Dukes of Granada, Estella; 'Captive Moor' carved pillar 12th C., *in situ* former Cathedral, Oloron Ste Marie.)

D: The Age of Alfonso the Wise, 1250–1300:
D1: Aragonese knight, late 13th century
This knight bears the arms of Tolosa quartered with those of Catalonia. By the mid-13th century a great deal of Spanish arms and armour was identical to that of Italy from where the kingdom of Aragon imported military equipment. In terms of costume, however, the Spaniards remained slightly different. A number of pieces of magnificent clothing and headgear have also survived in the tombs of kings and princes. (Sources: Sword of Santa Casilda late 13th C., Inst. de Valencia de Don Juan, cat. 56, Madrid; scabbard of Sword of San Fernando, Real Armeria, Madrid; sword belt of Fernando de la Cerda, Monastery of Las Huelgas, Burgos; 'Death of William de Montcada' and 'Conquest of Majorca' wall paintings late 13th C., Mus. of Catalan Art, Barcelona; *Chronicle of Alfonso X*, late 13th C., Monastery Lib., Ms. T.l.1, Escorial.)

D2: Castilian crossbowman, c.1300
Iberian crossbowmen were among the most effective in Europe. Those of Castile may have been heavier armoured than the *almogavers* of Aragon, this man wearing a cuirass of leather scales is holding the shield and standard of the knight. Certain details in the carving on which this armour is based suggest such protections were worn in Spain but could also stem from garbled reports of Islamic lamellar armour. The large shield or mantlet, crossbow and light sword are, however, more straightforward. (Sources: sword, 13th C.,

'Henry IV of Aragon', *Geneologie de los Reyes*, mid-15th C. Here the king is shown in light cavalry equipment *à la jinete*. (Ms. II-3009, Biblioteca Real, Madrid)

Inst. de Valencia de Don Juan, Madrid; *Cantigas of Alfonso X* and *Chronicle of Alfonso X*, late 13th C., Monastery Lib., Escorial; 'Gran Conquista de Ultramar' early 14th C., Bib. Nac., Ms. 195, Madrid; wall painting late 13th C., Mus. de Hist. de la Ciudad, Barcelona; carved figures, 14th C., *in situ* cloisters of Cathedral, Pamplona.)

D3: Andalusian nobleman, c.1290

Muslim Andalusian costume had been influenced by North Africa during the *Murabit* and *Muwahhid* periods while Andalusian military equipment was still comparable to that of Christian Iberia. Thus this man wears a full mail hauberk and mail chausses beneath his typically Islamic tunic. His sword is a late development of a typically Arab form while his bamboo-hafted spear and highly decorated leather *adarga* shield are in North African style. The gilded decoration on the front of his helmet appears in numerous pictorial sources and finds unexplained parallels in 13th and 14th century Byzantium. (Sources: Sword of St. Ferdinand 13th C., Real Armeria, Madrid; painted wooden panel and 'Conquest of Majorca' wall painting late 13th C., Mus. of Catalan Art, Barcelona; *Libra de los juegos* 1283 and *Cantigas of Alfonso X* late 13th C., Monastery Lib., Escorial.)

E: Civil Wars in Iberia, 1325–75:
E1: Portuguese knight, c.1350

Portugal was militarily old fashioned until the late 14th century, yet some of its élite clearly used modern imported arms and armour. This man is based on a Portuguese statuette which portrays an unusual form of great helm which includes a hinged neck-protecting bevor. Apart from plated leg defences he relies only on mail. In some Iberian horse-armours only the crupper or rear part was given a decorative heraldic covering. On the other hand perhaps only the front part included mail. (Sources: statuette 1325–50, *in situ* Capela dos Fereiros, Oliveira do Hospital; 'Portuguese knights' in *Libro de Privilegis de Mallorca c.*1330, location unknown; plate from Paterna *c.*1300, Museo Nac. de Ceramica, Valencia.)

E2: Navarrese infantryman, mid-14th century

Infantry dominated warfare in mountainous Navarre, an area which was also under particularly strong French influence. This man has a brimmed chapel-de-fer, a complete mail hauberk beneath a fully developed coat-of-plates which may be of Italian manufacture, plus leg armour of hardened leather. Unlike greaves of iron such leg defences were generally laced rather than buckled into place. The man's falchion is held in its scabbard by a buckle while his spiked axe is a peculiarly Spanish weapon. (Sources: axehead 13th–14th C., Prov. Museum, Vitoria; falchion from Puente Genil 1350–1400, Archaeol. Museum, Cordoba; painted retable by Jaime Serra *c.*1350, Episc. Museum, Vic; 'The Betrayal' wall painting early 14th C., *in situ* church of Urries, Saragossa; carvings 14th C., *in situ* Porta Preciosa of Cathedral, Pamplona; carved retable by Bernat Saulet *c.*1340, Episc. Museum, Vic.)

E3: Aragonese knight, c.1325

This man bears the arms of the powerful Montcada family on his shield. He is otherwise almost entirely based on the effigy of Don Alvaro de Cabrera the Younger, except for a helmet which is a form of early bascinet with a nasal. The heavy rigid bevor around his neck is supported by a collar which, like the upper part of his surcoat and his sabatons, appears to be lined with scales held in place by elaborate rivets. The extravagantly long cuffs of his gauntlets are probably of buff leather or rawhide. (Sources: effigy of Don Alvaro early-mid 14th C., Cloisters Museum, New York; unnamed effigy mid-14th C., *in situ* Monastery of Poblet, Tarragona; effigy of Hugh de Copons *c.*1354, Dioc. Museum, Solsona; wall painting mid-14th C., *in situ* Old Refectory of Cathedral, Pamplona.)

F: The Kingdom of Granada, 1325–1400:
F1: Mounted crossbowman, mid-14th century

Crossbowmen who actually used their weapons from horseback are a rare phenomenon but were seen in Central Europe and above all in Granada during the 14th and 15th centuries. Naturally this man uses a relatively light crossbow, his bolts being kept in a quiver fastened to his saddle. He is otherwise armed only with a large dagger and a light helmet. (Sources: 'Army on the march' wall painting mid-14th C., *in situ* Torre de las Damas, and painted leather ceiling *c.*1380, *in situ* Sala de Justicia, both in Alhambra Palace, Granada.)

F2: Qadi religious judge, late 14th century
Religious leaders played a significant role in the military affairs of Granada. Their costume was both more traditional and closer to that of North Africa than was the dress of the ordinary warrior. This man carries a decorated light sword of a typically Grenadine form, a weapon originally developed for light cavalry warfare *à la jinete*. (Sources: painted leather ceilings *c*.1380, *in situ* Sala de Justicia, Alhambra Palace, Granada; Grenadine sword 14th C., Archaeol. Museum, Madrid.)

F3: Grenadine light cavalry, mid-14th century
This horseman is equipped to fight *à la jinete* in a light cavalry style which, based upon North African tactics, was developed in Granada and was soon adopted by the Christians. His decorated helmet was probably imported from Mamluk Egypt as might his short mail hauberk with its stiffened neck. His leather *adarga* shield is of a North African form adopted throughout much of the Iberian peninsula but his sword is a thoroughly Andalusian weapon. (Sources: 'Army on the march' wall painting mid-14th C., *in situ* Torre de las Damas, Alhambra Palace, Granada; ceramic tile in imitation of a rug, from Alhambra Palace, 14th C., Archaeol. Museum, Madrid.)

G: The Battle of Olmedo, 1445:
G1: Aragonese light cavalry
Light cavalry in the Christian states of Iberia may have fought *à la jinete* in a manner copied from their Muslim foes but their appearance was generally very different. This man, for example, simply wears a small amount of normal European armour including a scale-lined *jacque*, a brimmed chapel-de-fer, plate arm defences without their associated gauntlets and a small mail hauberk. On the other hand his light spear, round shield, soft boots, spurs and horse harness are distinctly Iberian if not clearly Islamic. (Sources: 'Retablo de San Jorge' *c*.1420, Victoria and Albert Museum, London; 'Story of St. George' panel painting *c*.1420, Episc. Museum, Tarragona; 'Henry IV of Aragon' in *Geneologia de Los Reyes* early 15th C., Bib. Palac., Madrid.)

G2: Castilian peasant levy
Peasant or urban levies played an important role in the armies of all 15th century Iberian states. Naturally their equipment was often rudimentary. This man has a good quality chapel-de-fer helmet, a quilted or scale-lined *jacque*, a long-bladed *guisarme* and would carry a dagger. (Sources: 'Guards at the Holy Sepulchre' panel painting by Juan de Borgoña early 15th C., location unknown; 'Guards at the Holy Sepulchre' by Jaume Cabrera *c*.1400, *in situ* church of Saint Martin Sarroca, Penades; 'Catalan infantry in army of Count of Armagnac' wall painting late 14th C., location unknown.)

G3: Don Alvaro de Luna
Here the victor of the battle of Olmedo wears the latest and heaviest full-plate armour, mostly imported from Italy though with a French helmet. This is a great bascinet, a massive form of protection which could not turn on the wearer's shoulders. Such armour was used in Spain but never became very popular even among heavily armoured knights, largely because of the strength of the Iberian tradition of light cavalry warfare. (Sources: 'Retablo de San Jorge' *c*.1420, Victoria and Albert Museum, London; Great Bascinet, *c*.1430, Navarre Museum, Pamplona; 'St. George' panel painting by Huguet *c*.1445, Mus. of Catalan Art, Barcelona.)

H: The Fall of the Kingdom of Granada.
(Sources: these figures are largely based upon late 15th century carved wooden panels illustrating the Conquest of the Kingdom of Granada in the choir of Toledo Cathedral.)

H1: Grenadine infantry
Body armour seems to have been much rarer among the troops of Granada than among their Christian foes, though *salet* helmets were widespread. A few men also wore armour which, like the helmets, appears to have been of Spanish or Italian origin. This man has a helmet which has been decorated locally. His breast and back plates are from a captured Spanish armour and are worn over a *jacque* or coat-of-plates. The long-hafted ball and chain may have been a siege weapon while his slightly curved sabre probably reflected Moroccan or even Ottoman Turkish influence on these last Grenadine armies. (Additional sources: Helmet of Boabdil late 15th C., Met. Museum of Art, New York; 'Battle of Clavijo' and 'Scenes from the

Passion' engravings by Martin Schongauer based upon a presumed visit to Spain late 15th C., Nat. Gallery of Art, Washington.)

The main citadel (*Alcazaba*) of the Alhambra Palace. This part of the fortress dates from the 11th C. and it was here that the Spaniards raised their flag when Granada surrendered. Note a circular 15th C. artillery bastion added to the base of the old tower.

H2: Grenadine urban militiaman

It seems that every able-bodied man took part in the last desperate defence of the kingdom of Granada. This wealthy but unarmoured citizen wears civilian clothes that indicate just how different, and indeed how 'Spanish', Granada's costume had become compared to that of North Africa. Equally remarkable is the fact that such fighters still used slings at a time when many of their foes had adopted firearms. (Additional sources: Estoque (sword) of Boabdil, Army Museum, Madrid.)

H3: Spanish hand-gunner

This figure illustrates the degree of modernisation seen in the armies of late 15th century Castile and Aragon, now effectively united under Ferdinand and Isabella. Italian influence predominated and it was troops such as these who were soon to conquer a vast empire in the Americas. He wears a plated cuirass, including its laminated *fauld*, under a fashionably 'puffed' jacket and he is armed with an effective matchlock gun plus sword and buckler. (Additional sources: 'War-sword of Ferdinand the Catholic', Real Armeria, Madrid; 'Guards at the Holy Sepulchre' panel painting 1450–1500, Dioces. Museum, Barcelona.)

Notes sur les planches en couleur

A1 Equipment léger traditionnel qu'n'a jamais été complètement évincé par l'influence croissante de la France; l'écu rond, la cape rouge et l'épée légère présentent tous des caractéristiques musalmanes. **A2** Style catalan, semblable à l'équipement dans le sud de la France. Le casque à deux pièces tire probablement son origine des derniers prototypes romains; l'épée est de style musulman. Le pan à mailles sur la poitrine, rappelant la tapisserie de Bayeux, est représenté dans des manuscripts catalans: nous l'interprétons comme étant un *aventail* non noué. **A3** Des influences de nombreuses parties du monde islamique peuvent être retrouvées dans ces soldats; une cuirasse de mailles semblable a survécu.

B1 Des références écrites plutôt qu'iconographiques suggèrent des styles' d'uniforme sahariens très conventionnels. **B2** L'écu de cuir et le casque sont les seuls traits spécifiquement musulmans; la cotte de mailles a une forme européenne. **B3** Le casque est caractéristique des mercenaires chrétiens en Espagne; l'autre tenue est de style français, quoique plus légère.

C1 Tentative de reconstitution, principalement fondée sur une histoire d'amour andalousienne avec illustrations. **C2** Une caractéristique intéressante de cette tenue de chevalier est l'armure à plates portée sur le *hauberk*. **C3** Les sources illustrées datent de très tard; le casque est pris d'après une illustration marocaine, le costume des styles nord-africains urbains, mais l'arme est ibérienne.

D1 Notez les armes héraldiques de Tolosa et celles de Catalogne disposées sur quartiers alternes. Les styles italiens ont exercés une forte influence en Aragon, bien que des pièces de costume locales aient été conservées; quelques exemples ont été retrouvés dans des tombes. **D2** Il est possible que les arbalétriers de Castille, parmi l'infanterie lourde la plus efficace d'Europe à cette époque, aient porté une armure plus lourde que celle de leurs homologues d'Aragon; notez l'armure à écailles de cuir. **D3** L'armure est européenne, les vêtements de style musulman—même que ses armes et son écu, de forme développée. La décoration de casque apparaît sur de nombreuses sources illustrées; ses homologues byzantins suggèrent un lien non expliqué.

E1 Les chevaliers portugais, généralement vieux jeu, utilisaient des tenues importées de types modernes. Cet étrange casque avec bevor à charnières vient d'une statuette portugaise d'époque. **E2** L'armure à plates peut être italienne tandis que la hache est espagnole. L'influence française était forte ici. Notez les jambières de cuir. **E3** Notez les armes héraldiques de la famille de Montacada; Il est basé sinon sur une effigie de Don Alvaro de Cabrera, à l'exception du *bascinet* d'un modèle antérieur. La partie supérieure du surcot, le col et les *sabatons* paraissent être doublés d'armure à écailles.

F1 Les arbalétriers à cheval étaient caractéristiques de Granada à cette époque. Ils semblent n'avoir été trouvés qu'en Europe centrale par ailleurs. **F2** Les chefs religieux jouaient un rôle important dans les affaires militaires. Son costume est de style nord-africain traditionnel; l'épée légère de cavalerie a une forme typique à Granada. **F3** Le casque et le *hauberk* semblent être de modèle mameluki; l'écu *adarga* s'est répandu d'Afrique du Nord à toute la péninsule ibérique; l'épée est typiquement andalousienne.

G1 La lance, l'écu, les bottes et le harnachement du cheval sont distinctivement ibériques, alors que la *jacque* doublée d'écailles, le casque *chapel-de-fer* et les protections de bras sont classiquement européennes. **G2** L'équipement des recrues était normalement rudimentaire; cet homme est bien équipé, avec un *chapel-de-fer*, une *jacque* matelassée ou doublée d'écailles et un long *guisarme*. **G3** Le vainqueur d'Olmedo porte la tout dernière armure à plates, la plus lourde, d'Italie, bien qu'avec un casque français. La forte tradition ibérique de l'art de la guerre de la cavalerie légère empêchait une telle rumeur de parvenir à une grande popularité en Espagne.

H1 L'armure de corps était plus rare parmi les troupes de Granada que chez leurs ennemis chrétiens, bien que le casque *salet* ait été commun. Cet homme a capturé des plates de poitrail et de dos, portées sur une *jacque* ou une cotte de plates. Cet instrument à boule et chaîne à long manche pourrait être une arme de siège spécifique. **H2** Un citoyen riche mais sans armure prenant part à la dernière défense de Granada; il montre combien de styles lointains aux origines africaines existaient en Andalousie. Notez l'emploi tardif et surprenant de la fronde. **H3** L'influence italienne est forte. Des troupes telles que celles-ci n'allaient pas tarder à conquérir un vaste empire américain. La cuirasse est portée sous une veste moderne; ses armes sont un fusil à mèche efficace, une épée et un bouclier.

Farbtafeln

A1 Traditionelle leichte Ausrüstung, niemals gänzlich abgelöst durch den wachsenden französischen Einfluss; der runde Schild, der rote Umhang und das leichte Schwert zeigen alle moslemischen Charakter. **A2** Katalanischer Stil, ähnlich der südfranzösischer Ausrüstung. Der zweiteilige Helm stammt wahrscheinlich von spätrömischen Vorbildern; das Schwert ist islamischer Art. Die Rüstungsplatte auf der Brust, an den Wandteppich von Bayeux erinnernd, ist aus katalanischen Manuskripten bekannt: wir interpretieren sie als geöffnetes Aventail (Helmvisier). **A3** Einflüsse aus vielen Teilen der Islamischen Welt könnte man in diesen Truppen nachweisen: eine ähnliche Rüstung bleibt bestehen (überlebt).

B1 Schriftliche Hinweise eher als Illustrationen weisen auf sehr traditionelle Bekleidungsstile aus der Sahara hin. **B2** Der Lederschild und der Helm sind die einzige typisch moslemischen Merkmale; die Rüstung ist europäischer Art. **B3** Der Helm ist typisch für christliche Söldner in Spanien; die andere Ausrüstung ist franzöischer Art, aber leicht.

C1 Versuchsweise Rekonstruktion, haputsächlich beruhend auf einer einzigartigen andalusischen Liebesgeschichte mit Abbildungen. **C2** Ein interessantes Merkmal dieser ritterlichen Ausrüstung ist der schwere Plattenpanzer, über den *Hauberk* getragen. **C3** Bildquellen sind sehr später Art; der Helm stammt von einer marokkanischen Abbildung, das Kostüm von städtischen nordafrikanischen Vorbildern; der Helm aber ist iberischer Art.

D1 Siehe Wappen von Tolosa zusammen mit dem von Katalonien. Italienische Stilrichtungen waren in Aragon sehr einflussreich, obwohl auch lokale Kleidungsstücke erhalten blieben; einige Beispiele sin in Gräbern aufgefunden worden. **D2** Die kastilianischen Armbrustschützen, die damals zu der wirksamsten schweren Infanterie Europas gehörten, dürften schwerer bewaffnet gewesen sein als ihre aragonischen Gegenstücke; siehe ledernen Schuppenpanzer. **D3** Der Panzer ist europäischen, die Kleidung moslemischen Stils, so wie seine Waffen und sein Schild—in entwickelter Form. Der Helmschnuck ist in vielen Bildquellen zu sehen; sein byzantinisches Gegenstück deutet hier eine unerklärte Verbindung an.

E1 Die sost allgemein altmodischen portugiesischen Ritter importierten doch manchmal moderner Ausrüstungsstücke. Der seltsame Helm mit aufklappbarem *Bevor* stammt von einer zeitgenössischen portugiesischen Statuette. **E2** Der Plattenpanzer könnte italienisch sein, die Axt ist spanischer Herkunft. Der französische Einfluss war hier sehr stark. Siehe ledernen Beinschutz. **E3** Siehe das Wappen der Familie Montcada; davon abgesehen beruht er auf einer Satue von Don Alvaro de Cabrera, mit Ausnahme des frühen *Bascinet*. Der obere Teil des Waffenrockes, der Kragen und die *Sabatons* scheinen mit Schuppenpanzer gefüttert zu sein.

F1 Berittene Arbruster waren in dieser Periode typisch für Granada; ansonsten schienen sie nur in Mitteleuorpa vorzukommen. **F2** Religiöse Führer spielten eine wichtige Rolle in militärischen Angelegenheiten. Sein Kostüm ist im konservativen nordafrikanischen Stil; das leichte Kavallerieschwert ist im typischen Granada-Stil. **F3** Helm und *Hauberk* dürften mamelukisch-ägyptisch sein; der *Adarga*-Schild verbreitete sich von Nordafrika über die ganze iberische Halbinsel; das Schwert ist typisch andalusisch.

G1 Speer, Schild, Stiefel und Pferdegeschirr sind rein iberisch, wogegen das schuppengefütterte *Jacque, der Chapel-de-fer*-Helm und Armschützer konventionell europäischer Art sind. **G2** Die Ausrüstung für neuausgehobene Rekruten war meist rudimentär; dieser Mann ist gut ausgerüstet—mit *Chapel-de-fer*, gesteppt oder mit Schuppenpanzerung versehenes *Jacque* und *langes Guisarme*. **G3** Der Sieger von Olmedo trägt den neuesten und schwersten Plattenpanzer aus Italien, aber mit französischem Helm. Die starke iberische Tradition der Kreigführung mit leichter Kavallerie leiss solche Panzer in Spanien nicht weithin populär werden.

H1 Die Truppen von Granada trugen weniger Panzer als ihre christlichen Gegner, obwohl *Salet*-Helme üblich waren. Dieser Mann hat spanische Brust- und Rückenplatten erbeutet, getragen über einem *Jacque* oder Plattenpanzer. Der Morgenstern mit langem Handgriff mag eine typische Belagerungswaffe sein. **H2** Ein reicher, aber ungepanzerter Bürger, der sich an der letzten Verteidigung Granadas beteiligt; er zeigt, wie weit sich der andalusische Stil von seinen afrikanischen Vorbildern weg entwickelt hat. Siehe erstaunlich späte Verwendung der Schleuder. **H3** Der italienische Einfluss ist stark. Truppen wie diese werden in nicht allzu ferner Zukunft mit der Eroberung eines riesigen Reiches in Amerika beginnen. Der Kürass wird unter einer eleganten Jacke getragen; die Waffen sind ein wirksames Zündschlossgewehr, ein Schwert und ein Rundschild.